And when he had opened the second seal,
I heard the second beast say, Come and see.
And there went out another horse **that was** red:
and **power** was given to him that sat thereon to
take peace from the earth. . . . .

Revelations 6: 3 & 4

To Restrain the Red Horse

THE **URGENT** NEED FOR RADICAL ECONOMIC REFORM

Alan D. Armstrong

TOWERHOUSE PUBLISHING LIMITED

DUNOON, ARGYLL, SCOTLAND.

FIRST PUBLISHED IN 1996
BY TOWERHOUSE PUBLISHING LIMITED
GILNOCKIE HOUSE, 32 KILBRIDE AVENUE,
DUNOON, ARGYLL, SCOTLAND PA23 7LH

DESIGNED BY MAGNUS DESIGN, EDINBURGH
PRINTED IN SCOTLAND BY D & J CROAL LTD, HADDINGTON

A CIP CATALOGUE RECORD FOR THIS BOOK IS
AVAILABLE FROM THE BRITISH LIBRARY

ISBN 0 9529320 0 8

For Cindy, Angus and Mungo

I find, my friend ! that ye but little ken,
There's e'en now on earth a set o' men,
Wha, if they get their private pouches lin'd
Gie na a winnlestrae for a' mankind.

Robert Fergusson – *The Ghaists, a Kirk-Yaird Eclogue*

CONTENTS

FOREWORD

Ours is not a heroic age of social or economic philosophy. In place of Utopias or other grand schemes of reform, political thinking is dominated by the need to adapt institutions of government and society to the apparently relentless demands of a global market. Even the much touted New Thinkers of Left and Right – the technological conservatives, the communitarians, the "stakeholders" – offer variations on the global market theme.

Alan Armstrong's *To Restrain the Red Horse* stands well outside the current conventional wisdom and its franchised offshoots. It feeds on the same impatience with the market as such books as *The DEBT BOOMERANG* by Susan George or *The New Protectionism* by Tim Lang and Colin Hines. It identifies The New Economics Foundation in Britain and the Transnational Institute in Holland as fellow workers in exploring options for a radical transformation of the economic system.

Yet even in such company Armstrong's thesis carries an unfashionably prophetic confidence. For Armstrong is a champion of the ideas for monetary reform of American professors of economics, Irving Fisher and Henry Simon and of the even wider analysis and prescriptions for change advanced in the 1920s and 1930s by C. H. Douglas of Social Credit fame.

He identifies the cause of the multiple ills which afflict society – environmental degradation, the rising trend of unemployment and poverty, social breakdown – in the commercial banking system.

Through the fractional reserve principle Western banks generate interest-bearing debt many times more than the value of their capital deposits. As the servicing costs of this credit are absorbed into prices, society's purchasing power falls progressively further behind the price of goods, leading to recession and unemployment, the struggle for export markets and eventually to war.

Armstrong's solution lies in depriving banks of their power to create and issue money as interest bearing debt. Instead a state body, independent of government but operating to clearly defined rules, would be responsible for money creation. In the relevant financing period it would establish the total price of finished goods and services and the corresponding purchasing power available to consumers.

After allowing for the state's requirement for new money within stated low inflation targets, the state credit agency would issue the money necessary, debt and interest free, to meet any remaining overall purchasing requirements.

Whatever one's view of Social Credit and other proposals for reform of the monetary system, *To Restrain the Red Horse* provides a clear and forceful presentation of the thesis.

Armstrong of course writes from a Scottish context, though his thesis is very much a general one.

Over two centuries monetary reform, including Douglas's Social Credit ideas, have found champions in Scotland. Hugh MacDairmid indeed, with characteristic hyperbole, dubbed C. H. Douglas "the greatest Scotsman that ever lived". And there were many other adherents among the pioneers of modern Scottish Nationalism. Today the Social Credit Secretariat has its home in Edinburgh.

Yet none of this will make Armstrong's task of persuasion any less formidable in Scotland than elsewhere.

Armstrong's hope that voluntary organisations will join the ranks of champions of the sort of structural economic reform he espouses also has some way to travel. The majority of voluntary organisations in the United Kingdom still carry the ethos of their charitable origins. But he is right to detect change. Since the 1960s there has been a cadre of single issue campaigning groups. Now those voluntary organisations which are taking over some of the service functions of the state in such areas as community care, find themselves increasingly exposed to those financial instabilities which Armstrong attributes to the banks' system of debt creation. As a result they are being given a crash lesson in the economic and political realities of our "end of the millennium" capitalism. To embattled radicals, they offer up a tantalising glimpse of a civil society mobilised against its exploiters.

To Restrain the Red Horse is a brave polemic aimed at the heart of the financial system. Its boldness and clarity deserve a wide audience, its subject matter demands a critical one.

STEPHEN MAXWELL
EDINBURGH AUGUST 1996

PREFACE and ACKNOWLEDGEMENTS

The world is once again engulfed in economic depression. Its associated problems however are this time significantly more complex than we have ever before experienced. Together they now threaten not just economic and social breakdown, but the destruction of the human life support system. We have lost faith in the ability of economists, politicians, national governments and international organisations, to deal with the effects of the current crisis in any way which offers the prospect of a satisfactory outcome.

The result is widespread anxiety about the immediate impacts of our malfunctioning economies – large scale unemployment, new forms of employment with little security, declining social provision, poverty etc., and a profound apprehension about the prospect of ecological disaster.

Despite their continuing advances in the development and refinement of orthodox economic theory however, economists can provide no effective guidance on how international economies might operate **efficiently and with equity**, until they also are willing to deal frankly with the debt-money system which drives these economies. There are no signs, that without great pressure, they might be prepared to do so.

The debt-money system therefore – its history, operation and major impacts and reform – is the focus of this book. It is written in the hope that it might stimulate effective action and co-operation where currently there is not enough, so that pressure leading to prompt and radical reform will in fact ensue.

Although responsibility for *To Restrain the Red Horse* is wholly mine, I have been greatly helped by a number of people during the drafting and re-drafting of this book and I wish to thank them all. I must make specific mention though of Jack Hornsby who provided me with a copy of Thomas Robertson's *Human Ecology* and other reference material from which I have widely quoted; of Bill Hixson for his kind assistance in respect of material quoted from his own splendid books *A Matter of Interest* and *Triumph of the Bankers*; of Bob Good, Secretary of COMER in Canada, and of Bill Maclean for his help to a computer illiterate! Thanks too to my old partner and friend Roy Stewart who read, corrected and commented helpfully on an early draft and provided technical advice on the practicalities of publication. I am especially grateful however to Donald Neale, Chairman of the Social Credit Secretariat.

His experience of the Great Depression and its related agitation for monetary reform; his detailed knowledge of Douglas's Social Credit proposals; his correction of various drafts of the script and his constant friendly encouragement have all been very important.

Gratitude is also extended to the following for extracts appearing in this volume: *Triumph of the Bankers* by William Hixson, Greenwood Publishing Group, Inc., Westport CT. (c)1991; *Economic Policy for a Free Society* by Henry C. Simons, Cambridge University Press, 1948; *Economic Development In The Third World* (Fourth Edition) by Michael P. Todaro, Addison Wesley Longman, 1992.

Finally, if my tutors at Heriot Watt University, to whom I am also greatly indebted, should disapprove of this treatise I hope they will nevertheless approve of the spirit of enquiry which led me to write it.

ALAN D. ARMSTRONG
DUNOON SEPTEMBER 1996

PART
1

ECONOMY IN CRISIS

WORM IN THE ECONOMIC APPLE

INTRODUCTION

The 20th century is undoubtedly the most technically brilliant in all history and will bequeath the 21st century the most extraordinary legacy of stark contrasts. On the one hand we note the "triumphs of applied science in multiplying productivity in the provision of necessities, amenities and luxuries of all kinds; in overcoming disease and plague, and in facilitating transport and communications worldwide, even into space itself" (1), yet on the other hand it continues to demonstrate our astonishing inability to find a way of distributing the fruits of this great productivity with any generally acceptable degree of equity.

The effect of this disjunction is the repetitive rise and fall of the economic cycle and recurring deeper crises for which orthodox economic theory offers neither adequate explanation nor effective remedy. In the absence of such a remedy these crises continue to increase in their severity, and periodically they threaten the final collapse of the existing international economic system and the disintegration of civilised societies.

With each major failure of the system we are afflicted by a surge in the continuing upward trend in large scale unemployment; by widespread poverty amidst plenty; an ever widening gap between rich and poor; homelessness and crippling national and international debt. And yet to these and other related problems we seem unable to bring any effective solution.

Certainly after World War II, which finally brought the Great Depression of the 1930s to an end, the developed world enjoyed almost 30 years of prosperity and economic growth as the devastation of global war was repaired.

But these years were quickly followed by two severe recessions in the 1970s and the narrowly averted collapse of the international financial system in the early 1980s. Now in the 1990s – despite claims of recovery – we are afflicted yet again by an international depression that bodes this time to be worse than any so far experienced. On the occasion of each of these recessions and even more severely in the current depression, we note the paradox of growing poverty amidst plenty. Today surpluses of wine, butter and grain that filled intervention stores in Europe have been "dumped" in Russia and Eastern Europe while farmers are subsidised to curtail production. Huge numbers of unsold cars are mothballed and goods of every kind are piled high in warehouses because consumers cannot afford to buy them.

Suppliers of goods and services are forced to pursue ever more desperate measures to avoid bankruptcy by attempting to "capture" export markets, or by trying to clear surplus stocks on the domestic market in a frenzy of advertising, discount sales, competitions, "junk mail" shots and a host of other promotional schemes.

How are we to explain this astonishing physical and technological ability to produce an abundance of goods and services of all kinds, with our abject failure to ensure its effective and reasonably equitable distribution?

ORTHODOX ANALYSIS

Orthodox economics offers us a number of major "schools" of theoretical analysis of the workings of the system and then, related to each, a series of suggestions as to how it might be made to operate more efficiently.

THE CLASSICAL APPROACH

The Classical school suggests that money is at the centre of demand so that the ability of people to buy goods and services depends on the quantity of money they possess and, on the basis of the price level, the purchasing power of that money.

They argue that the Aggregate Supply function of the economy is "vertical at the potential for full employment" – that is simply that the total supply of goods is determined at any point in time by the combination of available capital, labour and raw material resources – while prices and wages are fully flexible.

If prices in the economy change, wages will change in the same ratio; workers will then be in the same position as before the price change and their willingness to work will be unchanged. And since this is true for firms as well as labour, the productive capacity will be unchanged and the relationship of costs to prices will be similarly unchanged. There will therefore continue to be the same level of goods and services for sale in the economy.

The supply function, while remaining "vertical" in this way, will of course shift over time as technology and improving skills and organisation of labour, increase the potential for greater output of goods and services.

The argument then, is that because both prices and wages are fully flexible up and down, if aggregate demand falls below the full employment level then firms will reduce prices to sell more goods. They will also however reduce wage rates since unemployed workers will be willing to work for less than the previously going rate, now that prices have dropped.

Aggregate supply and aggregate demand will therefore adjust to equilibrium again at the full employment level of output.

The outcome therefore is that market forces will automatically lead the economy back to full employment. Any mismatch between aggregate supply and aggregate demand will be a temporary phenomenon and there is no case for intervention by government.

THE KEYNESIAN RESPONSE

The Keynesian school do not accept that wages or prices are in fact fully flexible, at least in a downward direction. If the economy is shocked therefore from its full employment equilibrium (e.g. by the oil price shocks of the 1970s) it will not necessarily adjust smoothly, via wage and price flexibility, so as to return automatically to its former equilibrium.

Workers may accept a cut in real wages (e.g. resulting from a general rise in prices) for a time, but they will not accept a cut in real wages resulting from a cut in their nominal wages, as suggested by the Classical approach.

While accepting the Classical view of aggregate supply in the long run, Keynesians maintain that in the short run changes in aggregate demand may well result in a change in **both price and output**. It is therefore possible to have a short run equilibrium in the economy which is consistent with different levels of output and employment. This Keynesian analysis leads to the proposition that policies to manage Aggregate Demand so as to maintain full employment, can and should be used by government to improve the performance of otherwise "free market" economies.

Their view is that the private sector is inherently unstable and without government intervention to stabilise the economy it will be subject to significant "disturbances" leading to lasting deviations in real national income and employment, from those that reflect a full employment equilibrium. They recommend therefore active use of fiscal (tax and related government expenditure), monetary (money supply and interest rates) and/or other miscellaneous policies such as wage and price control, to achieve and maintain specific objectives for the performance of the economy.

The broad objectives of Keynesian macro-economic policy in this context include maintenance of full employment, a stable price level and balance of payments equilibrium.

If such target variables should deviate from desired values, then government might adjust fiscal policy. For example it might reduce taxes to raise consumer demand, output and employment, when unemployment is a problem. Alternatively government spending may be increased to create jobs. These policies would be reversed when the economy showed signs of "overheating".

Monetary policies on the other hand may be used to stimulate output and employment by increasing the amount of legal tender in the economy, or by reducing interest rates. Reduced interest rates would be expected to lead to increasing share prices as firms pay less interest on their debt to banks and consumers borrow and spend more. This in turn should lead to an increased willingness of lending institutions to grant credit and a resulting increase in investment and in due course employment.

It is assumed therefore that policy stimulus should be applied in a recession with high levels of unemployment and low inflation, while policy restraint is needed when inflation increases and unemployment is low.

Although the Keynesian approach dominated economic policy-making in the decades immediately following the second world war, there remained doubts about whether in practice its effect had been to stabilise or in fact, to destabilise the economy. A number of studies suggested that economic management was destabilising and actually aggravated the fluctuations they were meant to correct (for example because of time lags between legislating for policy changes and their implementation and subsequent effect). Experience of "stagflation" (simultaneous high inflation and high unemployment) since the early 1970s simply underlined this dilemma surrounding the validity of stabilisation policy.

MONETARISM

This theory, as in the Classical approach of which it is a development, sees money as central to macro-economic theory and policy. While monetarists acknowledge the need for careful attention to other determinants of aggregate demand, they maintain that changes in the money supply are by far the most important in determining nominal GNP in the short run and prices in the long run.

They agree therefore with the Classical approach in so far as they emphasise that governments should avoid interference with free markets, and should not attempt to fine tune the economy via Keynesian type fiscal or monetary policy.

They say it is unwise to effect policy changes based on short run concerns and instead advocate the implementation of a "Constant Growth Rate Rule" for the money supply. For example they say that a 2% or 3% increase per annum in the money supply (to allow for a similar growth in output) is compatible with zero or at least steady, low inflation in the long run and that further interference in the economy in the short run should be avoided.

RATIONAL EXPECTATIONS

Supporters of both the Keynesian and Monetarist approaches were subject to increased criticism with John Muth's introduction of the Rational Expectations Hypothesis.

This concept suggests that individuals use all available information and their understanding of how the economy works, in forming their expectations of the impact of any policy measure.

On average these expectations are correct because individuals understand and are well informed about their economic environment. They do not have perfect foresight but the mistakes they make are not made systematically.

When it is accepted that private sector expectations are formed rationally then they become an integral part of the economic model. If policy is changed therefore, expectations will also change and will affect the private sector's decisions about such variables as savings, investment and supply of goods and labour.

Robert Lucas, who developed Muth's original hypothesis, was led to propose that "fully anticipated monetary policy" cannot change real GNP in any regular or predictable way. If for example individuals with rational expectations expect that the money supply will be increased, then their expectations of the price level will adjust in proportion to the expected change in the money supply. Firms will expect that an increase in the money supply will lead to an increase in demand and prices, so they will be inclined to increase output.

But workers will also expect an increase in prices and will bid up their wage demands. The result will simply be an increase in the price index but no change in output.

Neo-Classical macroeconomics embracing rational expectations simply restates in a stronger form, the "natural rate of unemployment" hypothesis and concludes that unemployment cannot be reduced by the use of systematic government policy, whether Keynesian or based on the Monetarist Constant Growth Rate Rule.

The rational expectations hypothesis when first introduced seemed to demolish Keynesian economics. Subsequent work however has modified this view. In fact the neo-Keynesians too have embraced rational expectations while still insisting that, because in practice wages are indeed rigid (because of contracts, minimum wage laws, trades union power etc.), the neo-classical school's self-adjusting model of the economy is flawed. They maintain therefore that at least some level of government intervention can still be justified.

Essentially the only difference that remains is the view taken on the degree to which markets adjust automatically.

The important conclusions to be drawn from this truncated tour of orthodox economic analyses and their related proposals for the operation of the economy, is how singularly unsuccessful they have been in achieving their objectives.

Indeed Professor Paul Ormerod (2) observes that "orthodox economics is in many ways an empty box" and that "Conventional economics offers prescriptions for the problems of inflation and unemployment which are at best misleading and at worst dangerously wrong. Unemployment in particular **now represents a major threat to the fabric of Western society, and it is imperative that a better understanding of its causes and behaviour is obtained**". (emphasis added)

He goes on to note the pressure on academic economists to "work within the tenets of orthodox theory" and hints that he has been able to take a critical view of orthodoxy only because he has been fortunate enough to "combine academic research with a business career, which has removed the formidable pressures to conform which are faced by full time academics".

In reviewing Professor Ormerod's book *The Death of Economics,* Simon Jenkins (3) comments that "Economics is an accessory after the fact of economic crime. It peddles bogus objectivity, such as statistics purporting to measure unemployment or productivity or price inflation. It peddles no less bogus models of money supply, employment and growth... [and]... The only remorse I have encountered is from the Henley forecaster, Professor Paul Ormerod, [who] suggested that much current economic theory should be "abandoned or at least suspended until it can find a sounder economic base... If there must be a government economist, I say give the job to Ormerod".

Meanwhile economies remain unstable, subject to periodic cycles and, much more seriously, to recurring crises which increasingly threaten the final breakdown of the system.

It should also be clear that it is NOT simply a problem of political direction. As macro-economic theories have tended to converge so it has also become increasingly difficult to make any significant distinction between competing party political programs or their effects. In the mid 1990s for example Britain had had 15 years of continuous Conservative government (following neo-classical/monetary policy prescriptions); in France and Spain there had been extensive periods of Socialist government (following Keynesian/neo-Keynesian type prescriptions); in Canada the period had been shared between Conservative and Liberal governments, and in America between Republican and Democrat governments all following policies that can be identified with those broad schools of economics with which we have already dealt briefly. Yet in each of these countries we find virtually identical economic ills: escalating unemployment, increasing public and private debt, cuts in social spending in response to the universal cry that "we must balance the budget".

The knock-on effects include poverty, homelessness, loss of social cohesion, rising crime and Third World conditions appearing in the inner cities and rural areas of most of the industrialised world.

In none of the orthodox approaches we noted earlier however, and by none of the political parties, is attention ever directed unambiguously to the root causes of the system's failure. It follows therefore that they also show no commitment to the specific radical reforms which are absolutely essential if the system is ever to be made to operate efficiently and with a generally acceptable degree of equity. Even Professor Ormerod, in his criticism of current economic orthodoxy, does not touch on those characteristics of the system which are at the root of its failure.

By contrast, it is the objective of this treatise to highlight a distinctly unorthodox approach which will touch on these root causes, and in so doing will allow a much more realistic insight into how our economic plight might be remedied.

These root causes of system failure which, if left unaddressed, must lead to the eventual devastating breakdown of the international economic and financial systems, include:

a. Commercial bank creation and destruction of credit on the basis of the fractional reserve/debt-money system, which the whole world currently uses and which is simply unsustainable.

b. The impact of technology on the need for human labour in paid employment.

Between them, these two characteristics of the current system ensure that its operation must be accommpanied by:
* Escalating and unpayable international debt affecting National and local governments, business and households.
* Accelerating mass unemployment
* Gross poverty amidst plenty
* Increasing crime and trade in drugs
* Disintegrating social cohesion
* Global environmental destruction

Certainly in each of those individual problem areas much new thinking is currently taking place as a growing number of organisations are addressing different aspects – social, economic, ecological – of the global problem.

New policy proposals such as the pursuit of sustainable development, e.g. by accelerating the current trend from cars to bicycle transport and by increasing the use of windpower to meet the world's energy needs; mechanisms for relief of poverty and debt in the Third World; alternative economic indicators for the measurement of "wealth"; democratic devolution, credit unions, local exchange trading systems (LETS) etc., are being advanced, and the urgent need for this comprehensive or "whole-systems"approach is acknowledged in the strategy and plan for action outlined in Chapter Nine.

However before that, the argument developed in this book is that no matter how important and necessary these kinds of changes are they will finally have real potential to help resolve related problems, only if there is a parallel and **radical reform of the debt-money system**.

What follows in Part One therefore, first concentrates closely on a detailed analysis of the development and operation of the fractional reserve/debt-money system, then rehearses briefly some of its most obvious, direct and inevitable effects. It also deals, again in more detail, with the impact of technology on employment, showing why it exacerbates the system's inherent inability to distribute sufficient purchasing power to consumers, and so represents a further very serious threat to its survival.

Part Two of the book begins with a review of centuries of past struggle, and the growing current demand around the world for radical monetary and economic reform. It notes some of the very detailed proposals for fundamental change which have been made by major figures in the debate and presents a draft strategy to suggest how radical monetary reform, and the practical implementation of necessary and much wider socio-economic reforms, might in fact be stimulated.

Notes
1. Neale D.   1994 p. 5
2. Ormerod P. 1994 p. ix/x
3. Jenkins S.   1993 The Times 3rd. Feb

CHAPTER
1

THE DEBT-MONEY SYSTEM

THE MYSTERY OF MONEY

Everybody knows what money is, don't they? It is notes and coins, and the cheques and credit cards which are convenient proxies for cash, isn't it?

Yet very few people truly understand the "Money Mechanism" – ie how and by whom money is created; what conditions are attached to its creation; how it is injected into the economy; how the total money supply is expanded so that the economy may grow, and why it is periodically contracted with the inevitable corresponding contraction of economic activity.

The "peripheral field" of the money mechanism is certainly greatly complicated – stocks, bonds, junk bonds, swaps, discounting, futures and options etc., simply bumbaze the non-expert (and many an expert too).

Yet as Robertson (1) notes, the central principles of finance are not at all difficult to grasp. They can be understood he says "with less trouble than it takes to learn bridge or do a simple algebraic equation. . . The chief cause, however, for the closure of men's minds against any criticism of the money system lies in the nature of their experience of money itself. "

We all handle money every day. We recognise it as the only acceptable claim on some share of the goods and services produced in the economy; we save some of it for a rainy day in banks and building societies; we use it to secure our pension or to buy insurance for our old age.

But despite increased affluence in the modern world most of us would still agree that it continues to be scarce and hard to come by. To paraphrase the words of the Apostle Paul – no money, no meat.

There never, ever seems to be quite enough.

Its alleged "scarcity" is advanced to persuade us that housing for the homeless can't be built; hospitals and medical attention must be rationed; infrastructure projects postponed; student grants that reflect current costs of living simply can't be afforded, etc. No matter that there is available plentiful labour, resources and technique, there is simply **no money** with which we can ensure that what is physically possible is also financially possible.

Instead governments are always concerned that "we are living beyond our means". They point to continuing budget deficits and associated government borrowing in justification of swingeing cuts to public services, increased taxation and high interest rates, which they say will alone help us to get the economy "under control again".

Most of us find it difficult to accept this interpretation of events but we don't know how to challenge it.

The basis of this dilemma is again succinctly put by Robertson in his extraordinary tour de force, *Human Ecology* (2). He notes that the concept of money as being "tangible, real and substantial" is a matter of everyday and lifelong experience which conditions people to an acceptance that their whole range of activities, whether as private individuals, entrepreneurs or indeed as nations, are "crippled and curtailed by lack of money".

It is indeed "the final and unanswerable argument for men. . . "No money" signifies the shut door, the total impossibility, and in fact the absolute zero of action". He emphasises that the effects of such curtailment in the supply of money are felt not only by individuals, but by the greatest and most powerful nations on earth. It simply does not matter how much "of the earth's surface a nation possesses, no matter what size of a working population, no matter what available raw materials, skills or plant, or what her sovereignty in the extra-financial realm, the lack of money yet renders these assets as less than nought".

So where does money come from and who controls its supply?

Why can't we, as individuals or nations, afford to do what is socially necessary and physically possible?

Before we try to answer these questions it will be helpful if we can establish what actually constitutes "money".

THE DEVELOPMENT OF MONEY

Today economists and others are broadly in agreement with the definition of money as a medium of exchange, a "numeraire" or unit of account, and a store of value. Its greatest convenience undoubtedly lies in the first of these however as "anything which is generally acceptable as a medium of exchange or. . . is universally accepted in exchange for goods and services". (3)

So it need not be notes and coins which most people think of as money and which today are no more than the small change of industry and commerce. Before notes and coins in fact, many different things functioned as money – shells, tobacco, beads, dried cod, salt, hides, nicked sticks, etc. – and in some societies still do.

One of the earliest forms of more convenient "money" may have been dressed leather in the form of discs, with each disc representing a head of the cattle which in earlier times are said to have been "the common instrument of commerce". Homer for example is reported as noting that "The armour of Diomede cost only nine oxen... [while]... that of Glaucas cost an hundred oxen". (4)

In due course however a preference for metal money prevailed and it is thought that by 1091 BC., the concept of "cutting metals... (especially gold and silver)... into uniform pieces of specific weights and stamping them with their digital values led to the first coins which very quickly assumed the almost "universal" role of money". (5)

In later periods in Europe as economic activity expanded and in times of danger, gold and silver which served as money, and other precious items were often placed in the safekeeping of the goldsmiths who issued a receipt to the value of the deposit. It soon became evident that these receipts had begun to circulate and fulfill the role of money.

However as economies continued to expand, so too must the money supply expand. Such an expansion of the money supply however could not simply be effected by increasing the output of gold or silver at "the same rate that it proved possible to increase the aggregate output of goods and services of progressive domestic economies" (6) because of severe limits to gold and silver resources, and because of loss through wear and tear.

The loss in weight of silver coins for example, due solely to abrasion, was studied by William Jacob and C. C. Patterson. Jacob is quoted by William Hixson (7) as estimating that early nineteenth century British silver coins would "lose... 0.67 per cent per year", so that a given supply would be reduced to a half in about 100 years by wear alone.

However, as pressure to increase the money supply as a precondition of economic expansion became more and more great, the goldsmiths responded with great ingenuity and a new basis of financial credit was devised.

We have already noted that the owner of gold sovereigns which were in the safekeeping of the goldsmith found it more simple to hand over a goldsmith's receipt, now issued in convenient denominations, to discharge a debt rather than to go back and forth depositing and withdrawing gold sovereigns from the goldsmith.

In the course of this process the goldsmiths had also discovered that as their receipts increasingly circulated as money, and the need for money increased as trade and other economic activity expanded, it was in fact only very rarely that more than about 10% of their receipts were returned for redemption of the originally deposited valuables.

It gradually became clear to the goldsmiths therefore that they could safely issue receipts or notes up to some nine times the amount of gold or valuables in their charge.

This expansion of the money supply greatly facilitated the further expansion of trade and industry but in the process goldsmiths had become dishonest. The production of more notes, bearing their signed promise to pay, than were covered by gold and silver deposited with them was clearly fraud – they had begun the process of creating money out of "nothing" and in that process they were being transformed from goldsmiths to bankers.

MODERN BANKING

The modern version of this banking system had its genesis a little later, most notably in the formation of the Bank of England. It was established by a group of financial adventurers, including the "pre-eminent houses of finance in London's City... houses such as Barings, Hambros, Rothschilds" (8) and fronted by the

Scot William Paterson. After considerable political lobbying and intrigue they ensured that the Tunnage Act (also referred to as The Bank Charter Act of 1694) was passed by the Westminster Parliament. It was ostensibly a mechanism for alleviating the monetary difficulties of William III in connection with his need to finance the war against France and England's subsequent involvement in the War of the Spanish Succession, but in fact it neatly resulted in establishing a private bank monopoly in the creation of money (credit).

Indeed it is this authority to create money, granted to these private bankers, which has over the intervening 300 years been carefully consolidated and developed so that it now operates universally as the driving force of international economies.

Meanwhile, it was intended in 1694 that the Bank would attract subscriptions of gold and silver to the sum of £1.2 million – a huge sum for the times – which would be lent to the government at 8% interest and with a charge of £4,000 for expenses. In return the Bank was to be accorded a number of privileges, the most important being the right to issue a further £1.2 million in "Bank of England" notes which could be lent to private borrowers.

Christopher Hollis, quoted in *Human Ecology* (9) (emphasis added), notes that Paterson was perfectly frank in acknowledging that this privilege which the bank had negotiated was in fact a "privilege to make money". Indeed he wrote, that if the proprietors of the bank "can circulate their foundation of twelve hundred thousand pounds without having more than two or three hundred thousand pounds(gold and silver)lying dead at one time with another, this bank will be in effect as nine hundred thousand or a million of fresh money brought to the nation". In fact in practice they failed to keep a cash reserve of nearly two or three hundred thousand pounds in gold and silver and by 1696 they were circulating no less than "**£1,750,000 worth of notes against a cash reserve of £36,000**".

So there we have it, the creation of money by commercial bankers "out of nothing", and with a vengeance! Now it might be agreed, that while money was a commodity such as gold or silver it could reasonably be thought of as being in scarce supply, even when multiplied in this way by the developing commercial banking system. It is in this context of scarcity indeed that bankers justify charging a price, or "ráte of interest" (in excess of administration costs), for their supply of money. It is also of course in the bankers' interest in these circumstances to so manipulate this scarcity that its "price" might produce for them maximum returns over time.

We shall shortly see however that gold has for long been replaced as the base on which banks effect their multiple expansion of the money supply. The money base is now the notes and coins produced, at very low cost by government fiat, as legal tender. **There is therefore no inherent need for there to be any "scarcity" of money at all and so no need for a "price" to be attached to its supply.**

We shall see in fact, in the last part of this book, how an appropriate level of money supply might be injected into the economy debt and interest free! The only sensible constraint to the expansion of the money supply then should be the capacity of a community to physically produce

the goods and services which they consider are desirable.

This process, in which private commercial banks effect a multiple expansion of the legal tender money base and issue it **as interest bearing debt**, is of the greatest significance in any attempt to understand the causes of recurring economic crises and why, as individuals or nations, we so often cannot do what is socially necessary and physically possible. However before we examine the "mechanics" of this process in more detail, and then the nature of its long run unsustainabilty, it may be helpful to seek from a few other authoritative sources confirmation that will put beyond any reasonable doubt, its sleight of hand nature:

> I am afraid that the ordinary citizen will not like to be told that the banks or the Bank of England can create and destroy money. (10) Mr. McKenna, whose words these are, knew of course how banks created money, since he was Chancellor of the Exchequer in 1915 and was involved with the raising of war loans for World War I. He was later Chairman of the Midland Bank. Robertson notes that the "candour of his remarks is due to the fact that he was an unrelenting opponent of the present subservience of the commercial banks to the Bank of England". (11)

> Banks lend by creating credit, they create the means of payment out of nothing. (12)
> It is commonly supposed that a banker's profits consist in the difference between the interest he pays for money he borrows and the interest he charges for the money he lends. The fact is that a banker's **profits consist exclusively in the profits he can make by creating and issuing credit in excess of the specie he holds in reserve... and in exchange for Debts payable at a future time**. (13) (emphasis added)

HOW BANKS CREATE MONEY

Despite these unambiguous confirmations of this process of money creation by the banks "out of nothing", it is astonishing that so many modern economists can still be confusing, and apparently a little coy about acknowledging it in their textbooks or teaching.

Samuelson and Nordhaus for example, accept that the "banking system as a whole... creates bank money" but suggest that an individual bank "cannot do it alone". (14)

The proposition they advance here is that bank number one, having had deposited with it say £1,000 in legal tender(notes and coin produced by government) and using a fractional reserve ratio of say 10%, can now lend £900 at interest.

When this £900 is deposited by the borrower in bank number two, it can retain £90 and lend out the balance of £810 at interest. As this process continues, Samuelson and Nordhaus acknowledge that "finally through this long chain, all banks create new deposits of ten times new reserves" because, as Samuelson does acknowledge, when the first £900 is lent by bank number one there has indeed been £900 of new money created. The original depositor still has full access to her £1,000 of legal tender while the first borrower has simultaneously access to the £900 which has been lent by the first bank and which exists, having been created not as legal tender, but as an entry in the bank's ledger.

And by extension the second bank in the chain has created £810 when it retains 10% of the £900 deposit and lends out the balance.

Individual banks therefore, even in the Samuelson and Nordhaus scenario, do create money out of nothing, albeit at a rate only twice their deposits rather than by some 1000% by which the "system" as a whole multiplies the original deposit!

One might ask indeed how otherwise the interest on the total money created by the system is distributed to individual banks, if it could not be established how much each created.

The description of the process by Samuelson and Nordhaus might be thought to suggest that the creation of money by the banks in this way is just the fortuitous (for the banks) outcome of the system. Then, if the system were thought to be the most efficient way of ensuring an appropriate money supply for the developing economy, perhaps it is hard to be too critical of the banks incidental good fortune.

The authors of another major textbook, Paul and Ronald Wonnacott in fact seem to confirm this proposition. They rehearse essentially the same story as Samuelson and Nordhaus but add the comment; "In the normal course of their operations, they(the banks) create money. How did they acquire this almost magical power, and why should they be allowed to exercise it?... These attitudes reflect a lack of understanding of banking. There is in fact nothing magical in the process whereby money is created. Your local bank does not have a fountain pen with which it can create unlimited amounts of money out of thin air". (15)

Well, we may accept that they can't create unlimited amounts of money out of thin air but there can really be no question but that they do create very substantial amounts in this way. We will note later that as a rule bankers do in fact create well over 95% of the money supply which fuels the economies of all major industrialised countries.

Meanwhile, we have a very different interpretation of the money creation process when we turn to *Understanding the British Economy*. There we find that "The discrepancy between total bank deposits and the amount of currency suggests that the banking business is being conducted on rather reprehensible lines". (16) When the authors go on to suggest how the banks create money in a slightly different scenario from Samuelson and Nordhaus, they note that "although the bank **has not added to total wealth in this process, it has most definitely created more money by its operations**... (and they conclude that). . the essence of banking is thus to conceal or minimise the difference between currency and bank deposit... [and]... that so long as the public has sufficient trust in bank soundness, it will not bother to distinguish between cash and deposits. Banking turns out to be a highly sophisticated confidence trick". (17) (emphasis added)

Begg, Fischer and Dornbusch on the other hand, quite clearly do concede that "even a single bank can create money" and then go on to note. . . "However, this is nothing compared with the money that the banking system can create when they act together". (18)

But finally we come much closer to a reliable, clear and straightforward description of how banks create money out of thin air, and on a scale hardly hinted at by most of the previously quoted sources, when we turn to a textbook written for bankers and designed "specifically to meet the requirements of the Institute of Bankers Banking Certificate".

Hoyle and Whitehead consider in their *Elements of Banking* "a deposit by Mrs A. of a genuine sum of money, £1,000 in notes and coins". They then note that the possibilities are as follows:

a. We can lend £700 since we are keeping 30% of the deposit in liquid form (they are assuming for their example a fractional reserve of 30% rather than the 10% used in previous quotes) – this is the simple view of bank lending.

b. We can ask ourselves **"of what sum of money does £1,000 represent 30%? The answer is £3,333.33. It is therefore possible for us to have deposits of £3,333.33 provided we can find the borrowers"**. This is the sophisticated view of bank lending. (19) (emphasis added)

In fact, whereas the Bank of England until the early 1980s required all banks to keep a minimum reserve ratio of 12.5% this is no longer required. It is necessary only to satisfy the Bank that they are retaining a "prudent" or adequate level of reserves. It is probably safe in other words for the bank, certainly on the basis of the previously required 12.5% reserve ratio and with Mrs. A's deposit of £1,000 of legal tender, to have in fact total deposits of £8,000 and therefore lend to Mr. B. £7,000 which is of course "totally imaginary money created by the bank"! (20)

Let us assume that Mr. B. is a shoemaker who spends the borrowed £7,000 on supplies of leather from Messrs. C. who in turn deposits Mr. B's cheque with the same bank. It remains possible for the bank, from the original £1,000 retained as reserves, to meet any request from Mrs. A. for up to 12.5% of her £1,000 (i.e. £125) at any one time, and simultaneously to meet any request from Messrs. C for up to 12.5% of the amount of their deposit of £7,000 (i.e. £875). In fact, just as we noted in the case of the goldsmiths, depositors are unlikely to request the return of more than 5% of their deposits at any one time so the process is "really quite safe".

However if Messrs C. deposit Mr. B's cheque for £7,000 with a bank other than the bank in which the original £1,000 of legal tender was deposited, the cheque will be cleared through the banks' central Clearing House and Mr. B's bankers will have to pay £7,000 to C's bankers.

They have however in reserves, only Mrs A's original £1,000 and will not be in a position to meet this obligation. Any significant failure to effect payments in this way would undermine general confidence in the system and **would soon lead to its collapse**.

The dilemma is partially resolved by the convention requiring the banks to keep a prudent level of liquid reserves; to ensure sound security for loans, and to keep their lending "in step", i.e. in proportion to the relative scale of the bank's business.

Hoyle and Whitehead provide a simple illustration where we have a two bank system with bank A being four times as big as bank B so that the ratio of business is 4:1.

"Any loan made by either bank (i.e. any active creation of credit) should be spent by borrowers with the firms of whom four fifths. . . [will bank]. . . with bank A and one fifth with bank B. The money received by these suppliers will therefore return as passive deposits in this ratio to the two banks.

"As long as the banks keep their loans in the same ratio as the business they do, each will receive back as passive deposits as much as it pays out in active loans." (21)

There is however nothing here about the "long chain of the banking system". It is clear that the bank creation of money "out of nothing" is a function of individual bank size and not simply the inevitable and unavoidable outcome of the system.

An individual bank, operating on say a 10% fractional reserve ratio can in fact create, on its own, up to some nine times its original deposits and lend the credit created as interest bearing debt provided it "keeps in step" and can find the borrowers.

That the system will simply multiply this money creation still further is confirmed by Hoyle and Whitehead when they note that "Another aspect of the creation of money by banks is the extent to which any given overdraft will multiply up into further overdrafts to create further money". (22)

They go on to demonstrate this further creation of money by the same process outlined by Samuelson and Nordhaus.

So now surely there can be no doubt at all about where money comes from!

It might be thought that this creation of money by private commercial banks is not unlike the creation of illegal banknotes by forgers.

Forgers do however have to manufacture the printing plates, buy artistic reproductions of the legal tender they wish to forge and the right paper and ink etc., and of course they go to jail for a very long time if they are apprehended and found guilty.

Bankers simply use ledger or (today) computer entries.

And forgers are usually only concerned with the creation of money. Banks on the other hand, can also reverse the process! By calling in their loans, withdrawing overdraft facilities or selling securities "they destroy deposits – i.e. money", (23) and this is crucial to any understanding of the causes of the economic cycle which we will discuss later. So if the current banking system, and therefore the economy, is to have any prospect of survival there must be some attempt at firm control of the system and the money supply. But how to control it?

CONTROL OF THE MONEY SUPPLY AND THE BANKING SYSTEM

The following brief outline of banking regulation and control is related essentially to the British arrangements. They may stand as a close proxy however for the arrangements which largely hold good in most other countries.

At the apex of the system is the Bank of England, central bank of the United Kingdom. It is now nationalised but many of its basic functions are essentially unchanged since it first became the bankers' bank in Britain.

Because commercial banks operate on the basis of the fractional reserve system and thereby are able to create a large expansion of credit (money) relative to the amount of legal tender which they retain on deposit, there have been many occasions when public confidence in an individual bank's ability to meet demands for repayment of deposits in full has been undermined. The result has frequently been a run on the bank by depositors to reclaim their cash before the bank should fail. Often these have been serious failures that have threatened the whole banking system and the regulatory powers of the Bank of England have progressively increased as a result.

The Bank was nationalised by the first post-war Labour Government and its powers were extended further by the banking Act of 1979, and again by the Act of 1987 during a period of great turbulence in world banking.

The Act of 1987 required the Bank of England to establish a Board of Banking Supervisors with a view to further strengthening control and it introduced a general restriction on the taking of deposits except by institutions that were authorised by the Bank.

It does exercise considerable power therefore as supervisor of the UK banking system and in its attempts to ensure harmony between the objectives of government (as reflected in Treasury policy) and the credit creation activities of the commercial banks and other financial institutions.

The Bank of England is, inter alia, also charged with:

* Ensuring that the total of legal tender banknotes in circulation meets the needs of the community. It produces each week a record of the notes and coins in existance and the government securities that provide backing for them.
* **Operating as banker to the government**
The Bank maintains the government's account (and a few remaining private accounts). It acts as banker to the clearing banks and the discount houses and it deals with the accounts of a large number of overseas central banks and international organisations.
* **Management of the gilt-edged market**
Gilts are government securities which promise to repay with interest over a fixed period of years, or in some cases indefinitely, money which government borrows to meet its need for expenditure on its various activities in excess of that raised by taxes.
* **Acting as "lender of last resort" to the banking system**
Until the beginning of the 1980s governments required banks to maintain specified levels of reserves of legal tender. These reserves could therefore not be used by the banks as part of their money base to effect an expansion of credit. By increasing or decreasing the levels required to be held, governments had considerable flexibility in their attempts to control the nation's money supply.

However, with the growing influence of the new Monetarist approach to economic management and the related de-regulation of the financial services sector these mandatory reserves were discontinued in the UK and some other countries. Attempts by government now to control the money supply rely largely on open market operations especially via the discount houses to whom the Bank of England also acts as lender of last resort. This latter commitment reflects the notion that commercial banks, acting with due prudence, should not get into difficulties whereas the discount houses may do so from time to time.

The discount houses are bill brokers who will discount bills of exchange for anyone, borrowing and lending money in the process at low levels of interest mark up, often as little as 0.25%. They also deal with the Bank of England in the purchase and sale of Treasury Bills. In this way governments raise the short term funds they need and are also able to modify the size of the money base and so influence the scale of the total money supply. It is understood between the Bank and the discount houses that, although other financial institutions may bid for Treasury Bills, the discount houses will always ensure that the full tender is taken up each week. In return the Bank agrees to act as their "lender of last resort" if they should get into difficulty. This too is an arrangement by which government may exert some control over the scale of money supply in the economy. When discount houses borrow money for the purposes of discounting bills, they do so on an "at call" or very short notice basis. They must stand ready therefore to repay the money borrowed promptly, often with notice of no more than one day.

Because of this commitment, commercial banks can consider money lent to discount houses as being the equivalent of cash. They sometimes therefore lend at interest, their liquid reserves to the discount houses. The interest they receive is however much lower than might be had from general commercial lending, but since they may not lend their reserves to anyone else without jeopordising their "prudent" reserve ratio they are happy to have even a small return on what would otherwise be unproductive funds. However in the event of some loss of confidence in financial markets – perhaps because of some major international incident – banks may immediately recall their loans to the discount houses. The discount houses though cannot recall their money from borrowers because the nature of their business is to borrow short and lend long. They must nevertheless balance their books each day by 2.30pm and so now may face severe difficulty in doing so. In this case they will be "forced into the Bank". The Bank of England now acts as lender of last resort to help them out of their difficulty by lending them the money they need – but only at a rate of interest set by the Bank! In this way the Bank influences and attempts to tightly control the money market. If it is happy with the current level of money supply it may lend to the discount houses at the same rate as the discount houses have lent to the commercial banks so that they can clear their positions. If the Bank however wishes a change in the money supply it will set an interest rate on funds lent to the discount houses which will induce the desired change. For example, if the Bank is concerned about inflationary pressure and wishes to reduce the money supply in the economy, it will lend to the discount houses at a rate of interest higher than the discount houses have lent to the banks.

The discount houses will lose on their contracts with the banks and will attempt instead to recover their positions by raising interest rates to their own new borrowers. The level of borrowing is then expected to decline and the economy to contract accordingly. Of course the Bank may simply reverse the process if it seeks expansion of the money supply and economic activity.

However, despite the elaborate framework of Government/Central Bank regulations designed to control the banking system and the money supply, it is clear given the recurring threats to the system, that current efforts are far from being fully effective.

* International Representation
The Bank has also responsibilty for representing the UK in discussions, to try to bring control to the international financial system, with organisations such as the International Monetary Fund, The International Bank for Reconstruction and Development (more generally known as the World Bank), and the central bankers' bank, the Bank for International Settlements based in Basle Switzerland.

Banking indeed is now amongst the largest of the multinational industries and one of the most important reasons for its rapid development on an international scale has been its determination to evade such regulation and control. Banks have in fact "frequently moved abroad to avoid reserve requirements, deposit insurance, onerous reporting requirements, corporate taxes, interest rate ceilings, and other hindrances to their operations... [however]... While overseas offices may make banks more profitable by avoiding domestic regulations, at the same time they make banks and the banking industry more vulnerable and subject to crisis." (24)

BANKING INSTABILITY

Such crises were a feature of the pre-World War II period. They led first to the abandonment of the gold standard and the adoption of flexible exchange rates after the first World War, and then to the re-introduction of the gold standard in 1926 to try to deal with gathering inflationary pressures, protectionism and competitive devaluations.

None of these mechanisms were really effective and with the Wall Street crash of 1929, the world slid into economic depression from which it did not recover fully until, and it could be convincingly argued because of, the outbreak of the second World War. It was only towards the end of that war that the victorious major powers met in the USA at Bretton Woods to try to construct a new framework, replacing the gold standard (which had again been abandoned in 1931 by the sterling bloc countries), for the operation of the international financial system.

The major elements of the new system included the International Monetary Fund (IMF), whose operational arrangements have been changed over time to respond to fresh problems as they manifested themselves in the international system, and the World Bank and its sister organisations, with a remit of making loans specifically for economic "reconstruction".

Proposals made by the senior British representative John Maynard Keynes for a supra-national Clearing Union, or something approaching a banker to the world's central banks, were not accepted at Bretton Woods.

But in due course the Bank for International Settlements, whose existance had been threatened at Bretton Woods "because it had been too friendly to Hitler" (25), quietly survived with a low profile until it has now become effectively the Banker to the world's major Central Banks, albeit with a different nature from the institution envisaged by Keynes.

Yet despite these extensive attempts at international regulation of the international financial/economic system, domestic economies around the world continue to be subject to economic cycles that bring with them huge surpluses of unsold goods alongside mass unemployment and poverty, homelessness, crime and all the other socially damaging effects of the malfunctioning economic system with which we have long been familiar.

International crises still rock the system periodically and from time to time, and with increasing menace, threaten its complete collapse.

In 1974 for example there were the failures of the Franklin National Bank, New York's largest commercial bank, which made heavy losses from dealing in foreign exchange and the West German Bankhaus Herstatt which went into liquidation for the same reason, with debts of some DM2 billion.

1982 saw the collapse of the Banco Ambrosia.

In 1982/3 there was the international banking crisis that brought the system itself to the brink of collapse when Mexico, Brazil, Argentina and many other borrowers declared that they could not meet the scheduled repayments on their debts.

In January of 1995 a further Mexican crisis led President Clinton to arrange with the IMF and the Bank for International Settlements a $47.5 billion bail-out of financial institutions that had lent heavily in Mexico. This crisis was followed, just one month later, by the stunning collapse of Baring Brothers, Britain's oldest established and prestigious merchant bank, as a result of "unauthorised" dealing in "derivatives" on the Singapore money markets.

How can it be, that with all the intelligence, experience, expertise, supervision and control that international bankers and economists bring to bear on the problem, the economic system and the international finance system that drives it cannot be made to function without these recurring economic crises and the related massive social dislocation?

It must surely be that:

a. The system is simply too complex to be controlled in such a way as to ensure continuous economic stability with on the one hand growth, and on the other environmental protection and an equitable distribution of the fruits of economic activity.

and/or

b. There is at least one major source of instability which neither those who control the financial/economic system nor those who comment on it from an "orthodox" position are currently addressing.

What follows is designed to make plain beyond doubt that whereas the system is hugely complex and therefore indeed very difficult to supervise and control, or even fully understand, the second of these propositions is also correct and of infinitely greater importance.

The root problem is, in fact, the system of fractional reserve/debt-money creation by commercial banks. This process gives them a greater degree of control over money supply, and therefore economic activity, than any government, and they excercise that power in their own interests.

It is this mechanism that generates unavoidable instability and which ensures escalating unpayable debt, the cyclical nature of advanced economies and related unemployment.

THE WORM IN THE SYSTEM

We have previously noted the early connection of bank money to gold and silver, which was subject to significant loss through wear in use and to severe limits in terms of its availability as a natural resource. Eric De Màre notes in fact that "Throughout history no more than about 100,000 tons of gold have been mined and most of it is still around, about half of it now in the vaults of the world's banks for use in international exchanges". (26) [and that]... "In Britain the Golden Guinea maintained its value of 21 silver shillings from 1719 up to 1914, but by this date all the gold in the world would not have paid for the Great War". (27)

Gold therefore could not and cannot be increased at a rate similar to the rate at which economies might expand to produce goods and services. In these circumstances an economy will be static or in fact deflate if there is no alternative form of "money" which can be expanded as required.

The initial response of bankers to this dilemma was to increase their note issue relative to the amount of gold and silver reserves.

But of course there was a limit to this process too. Once they had expanded their note issues to the point where, for example, gold reserves represented less than around 5% of total deposits they had become very vulnerable indeed to any run on the banks.

In our earlier discussion of the Bank of England we saw how it was the intention in 1694 to operate on the basis of roughly a 30% reserve ratio i.e. that if the bank had "two or three hundred thousand pounds lying dead at one time with another. . . this bank will be in effect as nine hundred thousand pounds or a million of fresh money brought into the nation". However we then noted that by 1696, just two years later, the Bank was in fact issuing £1,750,000 in notes against a specie reserve of just £36,000 – i.e. operating on a reserve ratio of just over 2%. It is little wonder then that just two years after its opening, and not for the last time, there was a run on the Bank and it was forced to "suspend payment (in coin for its banknotes)". (28)

The continuing need for economic expansion and a related need for expansion of the money supply led in due course to the final abandonment of the Gold Standard, by which the circulating money supply had previously been tied to gold reserves. In its place was put a new money base which comprises "legal tender" notes and coins created on the instructions of Government. It is on the basis of this legal tender money that bank-created credit now rests. Essentially therefore the reserve ratio/debt-money system remains unaltered. Certainly, despite having given up a powerful tool in the form of mandatory levels of reserves, governments as we have seen do still retain some significant role in the control of the system, especially via open market operations.

Nevertheless, although governments exercise some control in this way, the multiple of the money base by which the commercial banks increase the money supply depends also on two major factors over which governments have little or no control, i.e. the willingness of the community, especially of business and consumers, to borrow and the **willingness of banks to lend**.

While the central Bank therefore may by its actions alone **shrink** the money supply, its ability to **expand** the money supply may in fact be significantly constrained.

Commercial banks on the other hand, have considerable ability to both **contract and expand the money supply as their interests dictate**. Very importantly they have also the freedom to decide where in the world's economies they may wish to invest, or where they might wish to refrain from investing at any time.

Therefore, since an increasing money supply is the sine qua non of economic growth, private bankers clearly exercise a very powerful influence over the **nature, scale and location of economic activity at any time**. Indeed it is the argument made here, that it is in fact the interests of private bankers rather than governments which ultimately determine the nature and scale of economic activity and which are ultimately responsible for the malfunctioning of the economic system. Mackenzie King, soon to become Prime Minister of Canada, could not have more accurately identified the problem when, in a radio broadcast on August 2nd 1935, he observed that "Once a nation parts with control of its currency and its credit, it matters not who makes a nation's laws. Usury, once in control, will wreck any nation. Until the control of currency and credit is restored to government and recognised as its most conspicuous and sacred responsibility, all talk of sovereignty of Parliament and of democracy is idle and futile".

Let us therefore now examine the major effects which follow from the commercial banks exercise of this great power.

We have established that of the total money supply in an economy, only a tiny percentage is legal tender and the balance is **bank-created deposits**. And although we have been discussing the money system in a UK context, this central fact also holds true in the context of the international financial system.

It can be readily understood therefore that of the total finance capital that fuels the world's economies, more than 95% is credit (interest-bearing debt) in the form of loans and overdraft facilities created by commercial banks.

If a group of entrepreneurs wish to establish a company for the production of goods or services, then start-up capital will be needed. In some cases this capital might come from the cash savings of those involved but in most cases it comes from public investment in equity via the stock market or by bank loans against security. What is not recognised however, is that it does not really matter what is the apparent source of the money, "it comes in reality and in the long run from the banking system which is the sole source of supply". (29) As we have seen, it comes into circulation as bank credit and therefore as interest-bearing debt. The problem however, is not just that in this way the banks exact a tribute from the community which they have no right to in equity.

It is also that the nature of this tribute ensures the instability of the system and in the long run, its inevitable collapse.

GATHERING SURPLUSES

Major C. H. Douglas (30) suggested in his famous A+B Theorem that in each production period it is not possible for the money distributed via wages, salaries and dividends, to purchase the goods produced in that period. The critically important proposition of orthodox economics that there is, in a closed economy, an "identity" between Income and Expenditure in each production period therefore does not hold. Certainly a further round of production, casting fresh purchasing power into circulation, can give temporary relief. But any subsequent round of production must result in due course, in a further increase in the total surplus stock of goods in the economy. The result is stock surpluses that continue to grow with each production period, leading to ever more desperate attempts to dispose of them in export markets and leading to trade wars and eventually to the build up for, and execution of military war.

The A+B Theorem has been vigorously attacked by orthodox economists, but if we consider how the generation of economic activity starts with capital borrowed from private banks we can see how his central proposition has validity.

Let us assume that the shoemaker in our earlier example, was previously operating on a very small scale but felt, that with the local development of a new industrial estate and related extensive housebuilding, there was now an attractive opportunity for substantial expansion of his business. He estimates that he is currently utilising only 75% of the capacity of his existing plant. With the addition of one extra worker and an increased input of materials he is sure that he can use his plant to its full capacity and in the new circumstances sell all of his increased output. He approaches his bank manager for loan funds of £50,000 to cover the annual costs of the extra worker and the purchase of additional materials. After discussion and on security of the shoemaker's house, a loan of £50,000 (created as we have noted "out of nothing") is granted on the basis that it is repaid over five years at 10% p. a. interest.

In the first year therefore the shoemaker must price his additional output of boots and shoes so that collectively they bring in £50,000 of revenue to clear his first year expenditure. However he must also repay in the first year, £10,000 of the loan plus £5,000 interest to the bank. He may also want a small profit on the operation even in his first year, let us say 2% or £1,000. The additional output therefore must actually be priced collectively at £66,000.

But the bank, when it created new money in the form of the loan of £50,000 did not create any new money **with which to repay interest or allow for the shoemaker's profit**.

There is in the economy therefore a shortfall in consumer purchasing power of £16,000 and boots and shoes, or other goods in the economy to that value, cannot be sold in the same production period.

THE GROWTH IMPERATIVE

Douglas maintained that the problem of gathering surpluses could be dealt with, in the short term, only by exporting them, selling them below cost as in bankruptcy or by instigating a further round of production which was not marketed in the relevant period. He insisted however that in the longer term the problem could not be effectively resolved under existing financial arrangements.

William Hixson captures the essence of the problem when he argues that in each production period there must be put into circulation not just current production and marketing costs, but that the costs of **new** investments must also be released into the economy so as to make possible the consumption of previously accrued surpluses. And that further, these new investment costs must be of a kind that give rise to no increase in **marketable** output during the time period in question. That is "They must be investments such as require a "construction period". . . before they become productive". (31)

Perhaps the best example of such "investment" short of full scale war is that of the peace-time military economy, the product of which never reaches markets but the incomes from which help liquidate surpluses as they are spent on goods and services in the commercial economy. In the UK for example many £ billion have been spent by government on maintenance and related facilities for the Trident submarine "deterrent" which, in due course and hopefully never having been used, will become obsolete and be scrapped.

Meanwhile the distribution of purchasing power, represented by the costs of the Trident program, will have helped very significantly to shift commercial surpluses wherever these costs have been spent.

In the commercial economy itself the Channel Tunnel between Britain and France is another good example of this process.

Begun in 1987 as a major Franco/British project the Tunnel was inaugurated on May 14th 1994, although it was some months after this before regular services commenced.

To finance the construction phase some £8 billion of loans and letter of credit facilities were provided by a group of lending banks and a further £2.5 billion was raised as equity. (32)

These sums were expended during the seven-year construction period in the form, ultimately of wages, salaries and fees to suppliers who used them to purchase goods and services currently available in the economy during that period.

The Channel Tunnel operators however, over their "Concession period" to the year 2051 must now recoup not only their current operating costs and profit but they must also repay their debt plus interest to the lending banks. As these debts are repaid, the interest will accrue to bank profits and the loans will be **cancelled in the "books" of the banks and removed from the economy**.

By the beginning of 1996 there appeared to be a real prospect that under the huge burden of interest payments on bank debt, reported by the Chief Executive as amounting to £2 million per day, Eurotunnel plc would fail. By October of that year an attempt to minimise that prospect led to a massive refinancing plan involving the lending banks taking a 45.5% stake in the company in exchange for wiping out just £1 billion of its debts.

But in the Concession or repayment period there will be produced in the economy (assuming no deflation) current goods and services to the value of some £8 billion, which cannot be bought unless there is an equivalent sum distributed as new consumer purchasing power, from yet a further round of production which is not designed to result in final goods and services appearing on the market in that current period.

It is this process that leads to the proposition made by Gorham Munson, and quoted by Hixson in *A Matter of Interest* (33) that "To enjoy the products of Factory 1, the public must build Factory 2, to enjoy the products of Factory 2 the public must build Factory 3 and so on ad infinitum".

Growth then is an imperative of any debt/profit driven private enterprise economy and if "what has already been produced... [is to be]... consumed, it is essential that investment should occur". (34) And if this unremitting drive for growth, involves regular and huge waste of surplus product, built-in obsolescence in even high quality goods, fashion goods and gewgaws that are designed to have no more than "life for a season", and most importantly an increasingly damaged environment, **then this is a price we simply must pay for so long as the debt-money system lasts.**

It may be objected that if profit and debt-induced growth is at the heart of the problem why is there a crisis of current proportions only now? The answer is that crises have in fact become more severe in fairly modern times because economic growth rates have accelerated dramatically over the last two centuries and especially throughout the current century.

Angus Maddison in his *Phases of Capitalist Development*, quoted in Ormerod (35), estimates that "in what are now the Western economies, during the 1,000 years between AD500 and 1500, GDP grew on average by only 0.1 per cent... [implying]... that in 1500 the volume of economic activity in the West was between 2.5 and 3 times as great as it had been in 500. To put this in perspective, the Western economies grew as much in percentage terms between 1950 and 1970 as they did between 500 and 1500. And given the much higher base at the start of the 1950s the absolute increase in volume of goods and services produced was enormously greater... Growth began to accelerate... [and]... during the eighteenth century... in more advanced economies such as Britain, growth was of the order of a full 1% per year". Today from a greatly increased base compared to that of the eighteenth century, we now seek average annual growth rates of at least 2% or 3%.

There are many people, especially those concerned with environmental degradation, who point to this need for continuous growth as the root cause of the global environmental problem and who therefore advocate zero growth as a desirable economic objective. Their concern is easily understandable when we consider the nature of exponential growth. If for example, an annual global rate of only 2% economic growth were targetted and met, then the world's total output would **double** in just 35 years and then double yet again in the following 35 years!

However, following radical reform of the debt-money system, the profit-driven element of growth need not automatically represent a threat to the global environment on anything like the current scale. Since we have begun to accept that neither a completely "laissez faire" nor a completely "command" approach can produce an economic performance that meets the approval of the vast majority of the world's peoples, there is now at least the prospect that we can reduce the need for growth as the need for profit is reduced. To do so we must ensure a more satisfactory balance between the private and public sectors, so that more relevant economic activity is undertaken by the public sector where profits are not the principle motivation.

THE DEBT IMPERATIVE

Restructuring the balance between economic activity in the private and public sectors however, will not alone resolve the problem of excessive growth. There is that other critical element – interest on bank-created debt which **ensures that without continuous growth the system cannot survive**. The elimination of this arrangement, by which money enters the economy only as interest-bearing debt, is also essential if the need for continuous growth is to be brought into a manageable scale. We shall discuss later how this can be done.

With a greater role then for the non-profit-driven sector and the elimination of interest as a condition of expansion of the money supply, it would become possible to ensure that such "growth" as is necessary for a healthy private sector is also of a sustainable nature.

Meanwhile, the result of this debt interest aspect of the current financial/economic system is not simply its direct impact on the need for continuous growth.

It is also that it leads inevitably to escalating levels of total debt in the economy and the indebtedness of every sector of society – local and national government, business and commerce, and households. As this debt and interest on debt rises inexorably on an international basis it eventually becomes so large, as do the undistributed surpluses of goods, that further growth of debt and output becomes impossible. The call goes out first for greater efforts to capture export markets, then banks fearing the prospect of widespread bankruptcies and large scale debt repudiation, withdraw overdrafts and begin to call in their private sector loans or lay claim to the associated securities.

Pressure is brought to bear on governments to cut borrowing and reduce deficits, in order to help "beat inflation". The result is cuts in social welfare and public services, reductions in infrastructure projects and /or increasing taxation! The money supply shrinks and unemployment and poverty levels rise. So too do homelessness, crime, drugs trafficking and abuse, and other effects that lead to a loss of general social cohesion.

We follow the cycle into its recession phase. No matter that there is available a plentiful supply of labour, raw materials and productive machinery to do what is both desirable and physically possible, it is no longer possible since there is "no money". There is no money because bankers have dictated, out of concern for their own assets and at times out of fear for their own survival, that there is to be no money.

The need to squeeze "inflation" from the system remains a priority despite the fact that, in circumstances of large scale unemployment and massive surpluses of unsold goods, it plainly cannot be a function of an "overheating" economy. In due course, when the recession has been in train for long enough to reduce accumulated surpluses and to mitigate the rising debt levels that have characterised the previous boom, the scene is set for a new round of expansion. So we endure the boom and bust cycle, which no orthodox attempts at stabilisation have been able to counter for long.

Yet despite the economic and social destruction wreaked by this process, and notwithstanding the run down of surpluses, the temporary reduction of private indebtedness by repayment of loans and/or transfer to the banks of assets previously offered as collateral against loans, or by loan write-off, the total of underlying debt continues to grow unremittingly.

Only private debt in fact has temporarily been substantially reduced by the banks deflationary action.

National and local government debts are never really significantly diminished by the process, and any drive to reduce government debt or borrowing requirement by privatisation of public assets to fund government activities, has at best only a marginal and short lived effect on public debt levels. Meanwhile, as the next expansionary phase gets under way so too does private (business and consumer) debt begin to rise again.

The underlying indebtedness of government sectors **despite receipts from massive privatisation of public enterprises** and consumers simply continues to grow. Table 1 illustrates the process.

TABLE. 1 UK. NATIONAL STERLING DEBT/CONSUMER DEBT: MILLIONS (SOURCE: ANNUAL ABSTRACT OF STATISICS 1987 & 1996 (Tables 16.3 & 16.4 and 17.14 & 17.19) and Blue Book 1995 (Table 1.1)					
	1976	1980	1985	1990	1994
Ctrl. Govt. Debt (St. £)	53,135	91,366	155,343	185,870	283,559
GDP(current prices)	125,247	231,772	357,344	551,118	668,866
Govt. Debt/GDP Ratio	42.4	39.4	43.45	33.73	42.4
Debt Interest+	1976/7	1980/1	1985/6	1990/1	1994/5
	4,449	9,732	14,046	17,730	21,334
Consumer Credit*	1976	1980	1985	1990	1994
Total Outstanding	3,423	8,291	26,049	53,488	58,344
Consumer Credit/GDP Ratio	2.7	3.6	7.3	9.7	8.7

+ *Each £2 billion in interest payments is approx. equal to 1p standard rate of income tax in 1996.*
* *Some change to series in 1987 but trend is clear.*

The process is not confined within national boundaries of course. More than 200 years ago Adam Smith noted that whenever bank created money exceeds that required in the domestic economy for "circulating the whole annual produce", the excess will be "sent abroad in order to seek that profitable employment which it cannot find at home". (36)

In fact the opportunities to deflect huge levels of lending to the third world, as industrial countries struggled in the 1970s with economic recession, simply accelerated the growth of international debt until it has become arguably the most conspicuous example of debt creation in recent years. It is this unstoppable escalation of total debt and interest on that debt, that currently most threatens to precipitate the (ultimately unavoidable) breakdown of the international financial/economic system.

Such breakdown may certainly be delayed, by massive bail-out arrangements to save overcommitted international financial institutions(at taxpayer expense), but it cannot be avoided indefinitely without radical reform of the debt-money system.

The signs are in virtually every country of the world, but perhaps most obviously it is the debt and debt service commitments of the newly industrialising countries which suggest that the next great crash cannot be far off.

Notes

1. Robertson T.   1975 p. 48
2. Robertson T.   1975 p. 49
3. Parkin M. & Bade R   1988 p. 70/71
4. Smith A.   1947 p. 20
5. De Màre E.   1986 p. 64
6. Hixson W.   1993 p. 9
7. Hixson W.   1993 p. 11
8. Engdahl F. W.   1993 p. 9
9. Robertson T.   1975 p. 64
10. McKenna R.   1928 p. 93
11. Robertson T.   1975 p. 55
12. Encylopedia Britannica   1929 Vol. 15 "Money" p. 17
13. Mcleod H. D.   1883 p. 357
14. Samuelson P. & Nordhaus W.   1989 p. 238/241
15. Wannacott P. & R.   1990 p. 195
16. Donaldson P. & Farquhar J.   1988 p. 197
17. Donaldson P. & Farquhar J.   1988 p. 200/201
18. Begg D, Fischer S, Dornbusch R.   1987 p. 489
19. Hoyle J. & Whitehead G.   1989 p. 19/22
20. Whitehead G.   1992 p. 369
21. Hoyle J & Whitehead G.   1989 p. 24
22. Hoyle J & Whitehead G.   1989 p. 26
23. Robertson T.   1975 p. 63
24. Levi M. D.   1990 p. 280/281
25. COMER   1994 (July) Vol. 6. No. 7
26. De Màre E.   1986 p. 63
27. De Màre E.   1986 p. 65
28. Hixson W.   1993 p. 61
29. Robertson T.   1975 p. 89
30. Douglas C. H.   1979 Appx. II
31. Hixson W.   1991 p. 19
32. Euro Tunnel   1987/94 Prospectuses
33. Hixson W.   1991 p. 19
34. Hixson W.   1991 p. 19/20
35. Ormerod P.   1994 p. 10
36. Smith A.   1947 p. 258/9

CHAPTER

2

INTERNATIONAL DEBT

There has been a long history of international borrowing and lending, and borrowing is justified by economists so long as it ensures economic returns greater than costs. However the share of returns which accrue to foreign lenders has to be in foreign currencies sufficient to cover repayment of both principal and interest. Relevant projects therefore **must result in an increase in exports or a decrease in imports by substitution or balance of payments difficulties will result**.

In the 19th century, in fact, much of the investment that went into the development of the USA, Canada and Russia was financed by international loans mainly from UK sources, and in the 1950s and 60s borrowing and lending was also seen as important as a basis for world economic growth.

Interestingly however, until the early 1970s it was widely considered that the "external debt of developing countries was relatively small and primarily an official phenomenon, the majority of creditors being foreign governments and international financial institutions such as the International Monetary Fund (IMF), the World Bank and regional development banks. Most loans were on... [concessionary]... low interest terms and were extended for purposes of implementing development projects and expanding imports of capital goods". (1)

Total developing country debt was in fact some $US68 billion in 1970, rising to $US180 billion in 1975.

However by the early 1980s new levels of international debt were threatening international economic stability and the very survival of the world's banking system. Although the commercial banks played by far the major role in the precipitation of this problem, there was also fierce criticism of official institutions, especially the IMF and the World Bank.

A short discussion of these organisations in this context will give a useful background to a review of the change in the nature and scale of international borrowing and lending that took place as the international commercial banks became more heavily involved.

It was at the conference in Bretton Woods in the USA in July 1944, that the IMF and World Bank were established. They were to be at the heart of a process designed to create a new exchange rate system, as the basis for greater international co-ordination of economic policies, and to avoid a repetition of the disruptive economic experience of the inter-war years.

INTERNATIONAL MONETARY FUND

The IMF came formally into existence on December 27th 1945. The Articles of Agreement required member countries (156 by 1992) to promote international co-operation; facilitate growth of trade; promote exchange rate stability; establish a system of multilateral payments and create an international reserve base.

Resources for the operation of the IMF were contributed by member countries according to a quota system, based on national income and the importance of trade to different countries. Of the original quota contributions, 25% was to be paid in gold – known as the gold tranche – and 75% in the country's own currency. A country could then borrow up to its gold tranche position without IMF approval and an additional 100% of its contribution in four steps, **each with strict conditions imposed by the IMF.** With the allocation of quotas went related rights, obligations and voting powers.

The IMF lending ability was extended as seemed appropriate: in 1963 the Compensating Fund Facility was introduced to provide special temporary help with short term foreign exchange needs, which might arise for example from some natural disaster like flooding or crop failure; Special Drawing Rights (SDR) were introduced in 1970. They are book entries, in a weighted mix of currencies similar to the European ECU. They are often referred to as "paper gold" since they were introduced, as trade grew rapidly, to supplement the original gold and Dollar deposits used to settle international balance of payments accounts amongst IMF members; in 1976 the Trust Fund (related to the sale of gold which was now no longer to play a formal role in the system) was set up to provide for special development loans. Finally, these extensions to lending arrangements were further supplemented in 1986 by a decision to allow the IMF to borrow, if necessary, in private capital markets.

In terms of member quotas, the IMF is dominated by 10 major countries which account for over 50% of total quotas, with America alone accounting for some 19%. This allocation of quotas is important because it is reflected in the voting power exercised by members of the Board of Governors, which meets in session only at the annual general meeting. Every member country has 250 votes plus one for each million of SDR, so that the developed countries, and especially the USA, have had a dominant role in the development of IMF policies since the Fund was established.

Apart from the "gold tranche" borrowing facilities were not rights. They were subject to scrutiny and to the attachment of conditions by the Fund's international executive staff, although since 1969 the first non-gold tranche, in addition to the "gold tranche", also became automatic and so not subject to challenge by the Fund.

The IMF therefore has adapted to changing economic conditions and to at least some of the criticism to which it has been subjected. One highly contentious issue however, that ensures continued criticism, is that of "conditionality" especially where it is exercised in relation to its programs of assistance to debtor countries with the most severe problems.

Whereas its original brief was concerned with helping countries resolve short term balance of payments problems and its role as custodian of the exchange rate mechanism, it subsequently and increasingly became drawn into involvement with assistance for countries with longer term structural problems, and especially those relating to international debt.

The rules governing access to IMF funds are related to the size, terms and conditions of the loans agreed. Conditions are attached in respect of how the loan is to be used and there is a review of a country's fiscal and monetary policies, performance of the exchange rate over time etc., to determine what the causes and duration of the problem might be. Then if the problem is seen as being deep-seated and therefore likely to be of a long term nature, there may be prescibed a program of policy action that must be followed.

The experience of Britain in 1976 provides a helpful example. In 1975 inflation had reached an annual rate of 25% and in 1976 was still running at 16% per annum. Government expenditure was also still increasing with a corresponding increase in government borrowing. There was also a gathering deficit on the external current account that was leading to pressure on the pound which government simply could not counter successfully. It was finally forced to call for assistance from the IMF.

Strongly influenced by monetarist theory the IMF, in a package of highly unpopular deflationary measures to be applied by UK authorities, insisted on devaluation of the £ sterling, severe cuts in government expenditure and penal interest rates.

Fortunately for the UK however relief came quickly when the North Sea began to deliver its oil bonanza. The balance of payments improved rapidly, in due course moving into surplus, and the £ sterling rose in the foreign exchange markets. The IMF loans were duly repaid and "sovereignty" was restored to the UK government. Needless to say however, the process was accompanied by much public disquiet at the humiliating experience of government direction of the UK economy being effectively replaced in this way by unelected officials of an international finance agency.

It is this kind of experience of IMF intervention which attracts so much criticism of its operation.

Its simplistic monetary approach so often involves the imposition of deflation on an already impoverished country; application of standard conditions that are not tailored to a country's specific needs; and an inevitable macroeconomic approach even when problems are in fact of a microeconomic nature. Such an approach is frequently totally unsuitable, especially where problems are deep rooted. It leads to a reluctance to turn to the IMF for help and problems often may be left to become much worse before they are finally addressed.

Another major, and increasing, source of concern by many clients and observers of the IMF is the degree to which its policies are directed by the rich countries of the North. Of the many interim and development committees, which advise the Fund on disturbance in the international monetary system and on fund transfers to developing countries, it is the G5 group (USA, Germany, UK, Japan and France) and G7 (G5 plus Canada and Italy) which are the most powerful. Ultimately it is their interests which are seen to prevail.

WORLD BANK

(International Bank for Reconstruction and Development)

The World Bank was also established in 1944 by the Bretton Woods conference. However its function is different from that of a normal bank and from the IMF. It was created to help encourage and fund post-war reconstruction by providing low-interest bearing loans for development projects, especially in the poorest Third World countries.

It borrows from governments, by selling its bonds to them, as well as on the world capital markets and offers loan assistance, principally for specific projects which must fulfill standard commercial lending criteria.

The Bank's lending is underwritten by its developed member countries. Together with its reputation for considerable expertise for assessing and managing projects, this ensures that it can borrow more cheaply and then lend at lower rates than those directly available to developing countries. Because of the nature of the projects it is involved with, its operational time scale is also much longer than that of the IMF and its loans may have maturities of as much as 20 years. In some cases, even this time scale has not been sufficient for some developing countries. In 1960 therefore, an affiliated organisation (one of four) – the International Development Agency – was set up to deal with those special cases by offering "soft loans" at below market interest rates on terms that could involve repayment over a period of 50 years or more.

The World Bank too however has been heavily criticised by some economists and by other observers of the Bank at work.

These criticisms take many forms, but are especially strong from those who deplore as irrelevant and inappropriate, the monetarist "free markets" approach to which Bank staff seem to have become attached, just as these policies have been adopted by the major industrial countries who also happen to dominate the agenda and policies of the Bank and the IMF.

Loud criticism of this kind comes especially from those who subscribe to the "Neocolonial Dependence Model", which "attributes the existence and continuance of Third World underdevelopment primarily to the historical evolution of a highly unequal capitalist system of rich country-poor country relationships... [and who maintain that]... Certain groups in the developing countries (e.g. landlords, entrepreneurs, military rulers, merchants, salaried public officials, and trade union leaders) who enjoy high incomes, social status, and political power constitute a small elite ruling class whose principal interest, whether knowingly or not, is in the perpetuation of the international system of inequality and conformity by which they are rewarded. Directly and indirectly they serve (are dominated by) and are rewarded by (dependent on) special interest international power groups including multinational corporations, national bilateral aid agencies, and multilateral assistance organisations like the World Bank or the IMF, which are tied by allegiance and/or funding to the wealthy capitalist countries". (2)

RE-CYCLING PETRODOLLARS

Yet we noted earlier that the IMF and World Bank had operated with some success and much less criticism from the time of their establishment in the 1940s until the end of the 1960s when international debt was not widely considered to be too great a problem. It became a major problem though, especially for the less developed countries, and began to escalate out of control as the world's commercial banks became heavily involved in "recycling" the rapidly growing funds of petrodollars in the 1970s.

On October 16th 1973 OPEC countries announced an increase in the price of crude oil from $3.01 to $5.11 a barrel. On January 1st 1974 the price was raised again from $5.11 to $11.65 per barrel. By 1978 the price had risen to $14.00 and by 1979 it had reached the "astronomical height of $40.00 per barrel for some grades of crude on the spot market". (3)

William Engdahl goes on to suggest that this series of price rises were in fact anticipated in May 1973, when "a group of 84 of the world's top financiers and political insiders met at the secluded island resort of the Swedish Wallenberg banking family, at Saltsjoebaden... [to hear]... Walter Levy outline a "scenario" for an imminent 400% increase in OPEC petroleum revenues. The purpose of the meeting was not to prevent the expected oil price shock, but to plan and manage the about-to-be created flood of oil dollars, a process US Secretary of State Kissinger later called "re-cycling the petro-dollar flows". (4)

In any event, by the end of the 1970s, as a result of these oil price increases, huge sums had accrued to OPEC members. They were deposited with the major international banks in London and New York that were dealing in dollars and in the international oil trade.

"Chase Manhattan, Citybank, Manufacturers Hanover, Bank of America, Barclays, Lloyds and Midland Bank all enjoyed windfall profits from the oil shock." (5) Simultaneously there was a co-ordinated approach to "deregulation" of financial systems by the major industrial countries. This deregulation involved, inter alia, either the removal or substantial easing of exchange controls, bank reserve requirements and other government restrictions on investment activity.

It was to this new flexibility indeed, that a number of commentators ascribed the avoidance of a worldwide economic disaster, as the offshore banking system proceeded to recycle the external surpluses of the OPEC nations with considerable efficiency.

Others might take the view that whereas the commercial banks served the OPEC countries and themselves well by recycling these proceeds from a massive transfer of wealth to the oil rich countries, they can hardly be said to have done many long term favours to the East European, Latin American and other countries to whom they lent, and who are now struggling under a weight of debt and interest on debt, which they simply cannot bear.

Difficulties therefore related to the current debt burden of developing countries grew very sharply through the 1970s as the debt and debt servicing (repayment of principal and interest) grew until it reached crisis proportions.By the beginning of the 1980s it raised a threat, as we have seen, to the very survival of the international system.

W. Cline (6) expresses well a point we have already noted when he emphasises that "because debt tends to grow at the interest rate (by "inheritance" from past debts, unless a country runs a trade surplus to pay interest), exports need to grow at least as fast or else the burden of debts relative to exports increases". A few developing countries, especially in Latin America had maintained overvalued exchange rates, which in a period of global economic recession simply made their problems worse. But most of the non-oil developing countries, who did not follow inappropriate policies, also experienced through the 1970s reductions in their export volumes and serious deterioration in their terms of trade. The result was, that the total of the external debt and interest on debt of the developing countries as a whole, rose from $100 billion in the early 1970s to over $500 billion by 1980.

The second round of oil price increases in 1979/80 led to yet a further sharp increase in debt levels. With this further rise of more than 150% in oil prices, banks were again awash with funds. The result was very low interest rates – in fact real interest rates in the UK were negative in the late 1970s — and the banks continued to pursue even more aggressive lending policies in the Third World. It helped the banks that easy domestic credit policies in some Third World countries, especially in Latin America, and the new availability of funds from abroad, allowed excessive public and private spending (especially on military equipment), just as the major developed countries were responding to inflationary pressures at the end of the decade by introducing stringent monetary policies and increasing interest rates.

Certainly most of the increased lending in the 1970s, in the form of petro-dollar funds via the commercial banking system, could be rolled over to postpone the pain.

But the increasing strength through the 1980s of the $US, in which debts were denominated, and the now rising US interest rates imposed further severe pressure on debtors.

The gathering severity of the situation led to fears that widespread bank failures would result from outright borrower default; that losses would be in excess of the capital base of many banks, and that the effects would not be limited to shareholders but would also adversely affect depositors.

There could be therefore a run on the banks if governments (i.e. taxpayers) failed to bail them out by purchasing their bad debts!

It was widely argued that any such bail-out would be highly inflationary and that the result would be financial panic and runaway inflation. Indeed the fact that the 1980s ended without widespread bank failures and international financial chaos is usually credited to the combination of the cautious and gradual, rescheduling of the debts; the co-incident economic recovery from 1982; and the remedial steps taken by international organisations and banks. Some of the most important of them noted by M.Levy (7) included;

- In 1982 an extension of $1.7 billion in short term credit to Mexico by the US Treasury and co-operation by other developed country governments in granting further loans to Brazil and Argentina. These moves, especially by America, reflected fears that a number of the major US banks who between them held some 35% of the developing country debt, would collapse.

- Between 1982 and 1984 the IMF and World Bank made $12 billion of stand-by credits available to the six largest Latin American debtor nations subject to adopting severely austere economic policies.
- In 1985 at the World Bank/IMF meeting in Seoul, James Baker, US Secretary to the Treasury proposed $20 billion of additional private bank lending to debtor nations and offered to arrange $9 billion of new loans from the World Bank and the American Development Bank.

John Denholm (8) however suggests that in fact the banks failed to make these new funds available since "the Administration was not threatening them with anything but rather making every effort...to guarantee their revenues... [and]... Banks are not philanthropic institutions".

Other actions involved Citybank of New York writing off many bad debts;an agreement by the G7 countries in Paris in 1989 to support the USA in easing Third World debt problems and the Brady Plan in 1989, accepted by Mexico and 500 creditor banks, proposing that each creditor could choose between :

a. Forgiving 35% of the Principal of old loans

b. Reduce interest rates to 6.25% or provide new loans.

Yet by 1989 the external debt of developing countries had grown even more to... **"$1,283 billion, an increase of 1846%... [and]... Debt-service payments increased by 1,400% and were in excess of $160 billion by the end of the 1980s".** (9)

There has been considerable debate about the real causes of the escalating debt crisis.Some commentators have blamed the debtor countries for indulging in "irresponsible" borrowing and some have laid a similar charge of irresponsible lending at the door of the commercial banks. Others have emphasised the impact of the crisis on the rising value of the $US, in which most loans were denominated, during the early 1980s and the high levels of real US interest rates that became a feature of that period.

But however complex the factors involved, we have seen from the previous chapter how this shift of resources to OPEC countries, in the form of petrodollar funds deposited with major American and British international banks, presented these banks with an opportunity for massive expansion of their lending "provided they could find the borrowers".

In the 1970s the developing countries – especially the newly industrialising countries of South America, like Mexico, Brazil and Argentina, and a number on the Pacific Rim – were growing rapidly while the older industrialised countries were still desperately trying to come to terms with the deflationary impact of the higher oil prices.

So that as the industrialised countries' average rate of growth was falling from "5.2% in 1967-74 to an average of 2.7% for the rest of the decade", (10) the newer industrialising countries were following expansive development strategies and were busy increasing their imports, especially of capital goods.

We saw in the previous chapter that continuous growth is absolutely essential to sustain the fractional reserve system. New borrowers therefore were essential and, fortunately for the banks they were now not hard to find, especially in the ambitious Latin American countries. In the face of recession in the developed countries and their very sluggish demand for investment funds, the shift of Eurodollar deposits to the oil rich countries must have represented a most welcome opportunity to the banks, co-inciding conveniently as it did with a situation in which although lending from official sources increased significantly, it was nevertheless still "insufficient to meet the growth needs of the middle income and newly industrialising countries". (11)

The commercial banking sector needed no further incentive to begin a program of massive lending to these newly industrialising countries, and other less developed countries, by their usual process of multiple expansion of credits on the basis of these new OPEC petrodollar funds.

Table Two illustrates the rapidity with which the growth of Third World debt and debt servicing escalated.

TABLE 2. SCALE OF LESS DEVELOPED COUNTRIES DEBT CRISIS IN $US BILLIONS. (Source : M.Todaro,Extract from Table 13.8 p.414) Economic Development in the Third World					
	1970	1982	1985	1987	1989
Total External Debt	68.4	846.6	1,016.6	1,194.8	1,262.8
Debt Service Payments	11.0	133.6	138.4	145.8	158.8
Debt/GDP ratio	13.3	31.3	36.6	38.4	34.5

Since 1989 total external debt and debt servicing have continued to increase, albeit at a slower rate. The IMF's World Economic Outlook of October 1994 (Table A.37), for example, projected that in 1995 total external debt would be $USbillion 1748.6 and that debt servicing would rise to $US billion 211.1.

Not only were the loans denominated in US dollars, significantly they were also made on the basis of floating interest rates.

Meanwhile, towards the end of the 1970s, the United States had become a trade deficit nation and suffered a net outflow of foreign investment. In the late 1970s the British and American financial/political establishments, together with many of the older industrialised countries, adopted monetarism as their economic philosophy and began a progressive increase in interest rates.

It was hoped in this way to attract investment funds from the rest of the world and boost their faltering economies. Interest rates in America duly rose to 16.6% and the value of the US dollar soared.

This approach had some considerable success as that capital which was concentrated in the hands of Third World country elites, took flight to safe, high interest havens in the USA and elsewhere in the developed world.

Anna Isla gives some idea of the scale and impact of this flight on Latin American countries when she notes that "the demand for capital in the United States acted like a vacuum. The Latin American elites began to send money abroad in ever increasing amounts... [and]... Prior to 1987, $270 billion was removed from Argentina, Mexico, Brazil, Venezuala, Peru and Columbia... This capital, which left the country, still appears on the commercial banks' books as loans on which the interest is due. So Latin American countries are paying off a debt on money which is in western banks being used to make more... (private)... profits". (12)

The burden of total debt and debt servicing therefore grew apace until they reached levels that the Third World countries simply could not sustain and as early as 1981 most new loans, most noticeably to Latin America, were needed to pay the interest alone!

As a result the money borrowed was simply returned to the banks and financial institutions as interest due on existing debt, and the total debt expanded by the amount of the new loans.

Faced with these problems the Third World countries had to reduce their imports and introduce severe IMF imposed stabilisation policies at the expense of their ambitions for further development. Alternatively many tried to maintain growth through further borrowing, or by a combination of these. Where further borrowing was sought it became usual that a deal had first to be struck with the IMF before international banks would agree to offer new loans or re-schedule existing ones. The deal with the IMF would almost certainly involve structural adjustment proposals which were designed to ensure that at least, balance of payments deficits would be reduced so that foreign exchange earnings could be used to begin repayment of previous loans.

Despite their efforts to conform to the requirements of these IMF structural adjustment programs, those countries that rely on exports of primary products like cotton, coffee, sugar etc., found themselves in a Catch 22 dilemma. The more they produced for sale on the international markets, the further the price fell and the less they earned. When they try to improve matters by adding value to these products by processing them they run up against tariff barriers imposed by the industrialised countries.

The results are devastating for the Third World. Anna Isla again records that in Latin America, "all social service provision and needs of the people have been subordinated to debt repayment". And where the IMF is involved in the search for a solution, "The SAP (structural adjustment program) dictates the national spending priorities and countries are forced to pay interest... [on foreign debt]... before health, education, housing and other development concerns". (13)

The outcome is widespread poverty so that "In Peru, Bolivia and Brazil, people... [are reduced to]... eating Nicovita (fish-meal used for fattening chickens) and wet newspaper, not because they are not producing food, but because they are forced to sell the food they produce to the North. Half of the population is illiterate or semi-literate, cholera and other diseases are spreading, drinking water is in short supply, and life expectancy is very low". (14)

It should hardly be surprising in these circumstances that IMF stabilisation policies are bitterly denounced as being designed to meet the demands of western financial interests, rather than the needs of the people for whom the loans were ostensibly advanced in the first place. Especially where further borrowing was part of the solution, the debt and debt servicing commitments escalated to the extent that in some cases, including such major countries as Brazil, Mexico, and China, it became barely possible to meet the interest payments on outstanding debt **from their total export earnings**.

The result is that the "debt burden has brought Latin American countries into submission, perpetuating a process of capital flight, impoverishment and environmental destruction". (15) A similar story of debt servitude, harsh IMF and World Bank "conditionality" with a resulting loss of control over economic and social policies to creditor countries and financial institutions, poverty, disease and internal strife, can be found throughout the Third World.

TAXPAYERS TO THE RESCUE

But what of the banks in these circumstances, where the debt burden had grown to such an extent that huge default was threatened and collapse of the world's financial system had become a real prospect?

After the alarm at the prospect of debt repudiation by Mexico and other major debtors in 1982, the banks began to retrench. They brought to bear all their immense influence with governments to ensure that the consequences of their excessive and ill-judged lending would accrue in large measure to the citizens, and especially taxpayers, of the rich industrial countries rather than to the banks themselves.

In most of these creditor countries, taxation and regulatory authorities have agreed mechanisms which allow banks to treat Third World debts as "losses" for tax purposes, "without any requirement to reduce the debt of the debtor countries on their books and, in some cases, with no actual cash loss suffered by the bank". (16)

The way in which the banks make use of these arrangements is by setting aside a "provision" against expected future losses from repudiated loans. These provisions are withdrawn from current bank income, thereby reducing profits on which tax would otherwise be due. With an annual profit of say, £600 million and a prevailing tax on corporate profits of say, 40% then by making a provision of say £150 million against expected losses, the UK tax authorities for example would gather some £60 million less tax than would otherwise be due. Government must therefore increase taxes for other taxpayers to make up this shortfall or the infrastructure or public services that £60 million would have bought must be lost to the community.

The big four British clearing banks in fact in 1989 alone **"made provisions" totalling £1938 million. The individual figures and percentage of outstanding debts covered by these provisions is as follows:** (17)

	1989 debt provisions (£millions)	Percentage of outstanding debt covered
Lloyds	464	47
National Westminster	395	48
Barclays	233	48
Midland	846	50.6

It is important to emphasise that the bank has not as yet made any actual loss, since the debts against which provision has been made remain outstanding and the debtor will be pressed for its redemption. Indeed in most cases shareholders dividends have actually been increased, in many cases substantially. Surely nothing could more convincingly scotch the myth, if it is still believed, that banks lend out only what they receive in deposits. Certainly if the debtor were a business which was bankrupted, these provisions would then be set against the write-off of the loan but even then the bank's "losses" would have already been mitigated by tax relief.

On the other hand where tax provisions are permitted, as they are in most countries, and when the debtor is a sovereign government, the provisions can be maintained for years while the loan also remains on the books of the bank. John Denholm (18) notes that the British private banking analysts IBCA suggest, that "Using a 35% tax rate, the Inland Revenue will bear about $US7 billion of the $US20 billion of provisions". In addition to tax relief for "provisions" against expected bad debt, banks may also obtain tax concessions to help them extricate themselves from their own debt crisis by dealing in a secondary market for loans. There, loans are bought and sold and a banker concerned that there is a real prospect that a debt will be repudiated, may try to sell it to another banker. If the second banker takes a more optimistic view about the prospect of recovering at least part of the debt, he may buy the loan at a discount which reflects his own view of the risk of default. The first banker is then making a loss on his loan and will receive a tax concession on the amount of the loss. Meanwhile the debtor gets no relief and again the loan remains outstanding, though now it would appear on the books of a different bank!

The secondary market exists because participants take different views about the degree of risk of eventual default and because experience confirms that the risk taken by buyers of second hand debt is often well rewarded.

The cost to taxpayers of the "creditor countries" is estimated as being very large indeed. Denholm (19) using World Bank data for selected OECD countries in 1984 and 1990, noted that the banks had managed to reduce substantially their "outstanding debts held by them on the dangerous SIMIC's". SIMIC's are "Severely Indebted Middle Income Countries" i.e. those affording most risk to creditors. In summarising the approach taken in the major OECD countries to tax relief for banks' provisions against likely debt default, he refers to the total of probable tax credits against loan loss provisions obtained by banks in major OECD creditor countries in 1987-1990 and suggests that quite literally in the period from 1987 until mid 1990, taxpayers of North America and Europe provided their banks with "a rock bottom figure of $40 billion in tax relief". So that we might be able to grasp the magnitude of such a sum, he goes on to put it into a more easily understood context. It is he suggests greatly in excess of the Gross National Product of virtually any Third World country with the exception perhaps of the very biggest ones like India or China and is some "55 times UNICEF's budget for 1990... [or]... is much more than the $34 billion of Official Development Assistance (ODA) accorded to all developing countries in 1987". (20)

In addition we noted earlier the phenomenon of capital flight from debtor countries as ruling elites export their accummulated claims on wealth to the USA and other industrial country safe havens to escape the prospect of devaluation resulting from IMF imposed structural adjustment programs, and to earn high rates of interest. Capital flight is of great advantage to bankers, but exacerbates the difficulties with which the Third World countries have to contend, and places a further burden on Northern taxpayers where governments do not tax earnings belonging to foreign nationals.

Denholm (21) concludes his look at "bailing out the bankers" by suggesting that "·Northern taxpayers have contributed to banks, or simply lost" :

- Between $44 and $50 billion in tax relief on bank provisions and losses...
  At least $33 billion – far more when World Bank and IMF Capital Increases are counted – in disguised subsidies·from public entities to private banks...
- A minimum of $8-10 billion a year in taxes foregone on capital flight, or some $80 billion for the decade.

Strangely enough this huge shift of the debt burden from the commercial banks to the public sector has so far been the subject of very little public comment.

The banks seem to have extricated themselves from the folly of their lending policies of the 1970s and simultaneously to have avoided the criticism that might be thought their due. Meanwhile the Third World's debts are still outstanding and Northern taxpayers have funded a major bank rescue mission!

IBCA Banking Analysis Ltd., quoted in *The DEBT BOOMERANG*, said in February 1990 that they had **"no doubt that most of the pain associated with LDC lending is now history as far as the banks are concerned"**. (22) (emphasis added)

For the first time however more than half of the Third World debt is held by the IMF, World Bank and other official lenders of the industrialised countries. It is expected that this process is likely to continue as "the risk of lending money to the poor countries is being transferred from commercial bank stockholders to the backs of taxpayers". (23)

It is little wonder therefore, that western governments of every political persuasion are under severe pressure from their financial mentors to make swingeing cuts to public services, reduce their borrowing requirements and increase taxation so that they can "balance their budgets".

We observed in the last chapter how the debt-money system made continuous economic growth an absolute imperative; how it also ensured a chronic shortage of consumer purchasing power so that the fruits of that growth could not be distributed with efficiency or equity, and how between them these failings lead to growing levels of debt, enormous waste and environmental damage.

The impact of these characteristics of the system on the Third World has been made especially clear. Its effects in the form of debt enslavement, desperate poverty and especially the catastrophic destruction of their rain forests and associated biological diversity, are now almost universally understood. These effects have done much to ensure that environmental issues too are now of huge international concern, and it is to this impact of the current financial system on the global environment to which we now turn.

Notes

1. Todaro M.P.   1989 p. 411
2. Todaro M.P.   1989 p. 78/79
3. Engdahl F.W.   1993 p. 193
4. Engdahl F.W.   1993 p. 149
5. Engdahl F.W.   1993 p. 155
6. Cline W.R.   1985
7. Levi M.D.   1990 p. 513
8. George S.   1992 p. 89
9. Todaro M.P.   1989 p. 413/415
10. Todaro M.P.   1989 p. 415
11. Todaro M.P.   1989 p. 415
12. Isla A.   1993
13. Isla A.   1993
14. Isla A.   1993
15. Isla A.   1993
16. George S.   1992 p. 65
17. The Social Crediter   1989 p. 22
18. George S.   1992 p. 79
19. George S.   1992 p. 72
20. George S.   1992 p. 82/83
21. George S.   1992 p. 91/92
22. George S.   1992 p. 84
23. George S.   1992 p. 86/87

CHAPTER

3

ENVIRONMENTAL IMPACT

That there is a major environmental problem on a global basis is surely no longer subject to serious doubt.It has however been a long road to the Rio Summit of June 1992.

International acknowledgement of the seriousness of the problem was then reflected in the "Principles" adopted in the *Rio Declaration on Environment* and Development. Numbers 4 and 7 respectively read:

> In order to achieve sustainable development, environmental protection shall constitute an integral part of the development process and cannot be considered in isolation from it.

and

> States shall co-operate in a spirit of global partnership to conserve, protect and restore the health and integrity of the Earth's ecosytem. In view of the different contributions to global environmental degradation, States have common but different responsibilities. The developed countries acknowledge the responsibilty that they bear in the international pursuit of sustainable development in view of the pressures their societies place on the global environment and of the technologies and financial resources they command.

However what must remain open to doubt, is that these ringing declarations of commitment to sustainable development will actually be translated into effective action.

Demand by the world's people for economic growth so that they might enjoy higher living standards leads politicians and even many environmentalists to continue to link talk of sustainable development, sustainable growth and sustainable progress as though they are interchangeable and can actually be achieved.Yet while accepting that growth could be achieved with much less damage to the environment than is currently the case, they must be aware that **sustainable growth is in fact a contradiction in terms. It implies progress on a path towards infinite growth in a finite world and is therefore clearly NOT sustainable**.

On the other hand, whereas **sustainable development** may be thought an acceptable alternative because it involves a different approach to the concept of growth and a positive concern for the survival and renewal of the natural environment, it is in turn incompatible with the current financial system which absolutely **must** have exponential growth if bank loans and related interest payments are to be recovered by the banking system.

Neither does it encourage any expectation of prompt action when we reflect that concern and debate about the impact of economic growth on the world's environment goes back at least as far as the work of Thomas Malthus (1766-1834).

THE GATHERING DEBATE

Arguing that there was a direct relationship between population growth and environmental damage, Malthus suggested that the supply of land was finite. Agricultural productivity could not continue indefinitely since there were declining returns to agricultural inputs. Population would always grow at a faster rate than food supply. The resulting imbalance between population growth and available resources would lead to such stress on resources that equilibrium could only be restored after famine, war or "vice" (by which he meant population control through contraception, abortion or infanticide).

Already the argument was couched in terms of growth versus environment. But Malthus had not foreseen the enormous advance in technologies that would, at least temporarily, overcome diminishing returns. As a result, the excitement and optimism that came with this technological and industrial revolution banished, for almost two centuries, such "dismal" forecasts about the eventual impact of continuous growth.

Indeed in the early 1960s, many people in the industrial world were still enjoying the thought that they "had never had it so good". The re-construction of post-war Europe was continuing apace and the Keynesian prescription, involving government intervention, seemed finally to have solved the economic problem as it delivered growth, stability and full employment. There was little thought that if such growing prosperity were to continue, it might be enjoyed only at significant cost to the global environment.

There were some however, even then, who were not so sanguine about the prospect of maintaining current levels of growth and prosperity for long. In 1966 Professor Kenneth Boulding contributed a more sobering note in his essay *The economics of the coming spaceship Earth* when he proposed that, "We are now in the middle of a long process of transition in the nature of the image which man has of himself and of his environment". He touched on a number of problems – the "closed" nature of the Earth's systems; the temporary nature of energy inputs from fossil fuels; current attitudes to consumption and growth which often suggest that the "future should be left to the future" etc. He concluded hopefully however that "it may be true that a long run vision, as it were, of the deep crisis that faces mankind may predispose people to take more interest in the immediate problems and devote more effort to their solutions". (2)

In 1969 E. J. Mishan in his book *The Costs of Economic Growth* took a less sanguine view, commenting that "Though no economist who had studied the relations between economics and social welfare would endorse a policy of economic growth without an embarrassing amount of qualification, the profession as a whole behaves as if, on balance, it was a good thing... [and... The belief that faster economic growth will enable any country to "pay its way in the world", or that faster growth generates more exports, hardly stands analysis... The simple view that it enriches society, or that it expands the range of choice open to mankind, stands up neither to argument nor to the facts of common experience". (3)

Then, when in 1972 the Club of Rome published *The Limits to Growth*, the report of a team led by Professor Dennis Meadows of the Massachusetts Institute of Technology, its three major conclusions were:

- If the present growth trends in world population, industrialisation, pollution, and resource depletion continue unchanged, the limits to growth on this planet will be reached some time within the next one hundred years. The most probable result will be a rather sudden and uncontrollable decline in both population and industrial capacity.
- It is possible to alter these growth trends and to establish a condition of ecological and economic stability that is sustainable far into the future. The state of global equilibrium could be designed so that basic material needs of each person on earth are satisfied and each person has an equal opportunity to realise his/her individual potential.
- If the world's people decide to strive for this second outcome rather than the first, the sooner they begin working to attain it the greater will be their chances of success. (4)

The report was "debated by parliaments and scientific societies... [and it]... inspired some high praise... and a **flurry of attacks from the left, the right and the middle of mainstream economics**." (5)

Most of this critical attention however was paid to the first of these conclusions, leading critics to suggest that the report was, in line with the "growth versus environment" approach, advocating zero growth and that this must be unacceptable to all those who were concerned about the plight of the peoples of the Third World.

In fact the Club of Rome in its own subsequent report *The First Global Revolution*, makes it plain that this was never their conviction.

They fully accepted the need for growth in poor countries of the world while warning of the potential consequences of any pursuit of indiscriminate growth by the industrialised countries.

The original authors of *The Limits to Growth* report insist in their sequel *Beyond the Limits*, that whereas "The book was interpreted by many as a prediction of doom... it was not a prediction at all. It was about choice. It contained a warning to be sure, but also a message of promise". (6)

The *Limits* team had been aware from the beginning that their conclusions would be a matter of heated debate – indeed they positively welcomed it. In their introduction to the original report they emphasised that part of their purpose was in fact to open that debate, and in this they were successful.

It was however 1980 before the World Conservation Strategy (of the International Union for Conservation of Nature and Natural Resources) introduced the idea of integrating development and the environment with a view to achieving "sustainable development". This idea of sustainable development was then more firmly established as an alternative approach to the issue when, seven years later, the World Commission on Environment and Development, chaired by the Norwegian Prime Minister Gro Bruntland, published its report *Our Common Future*. That report called for an integrated approach to economic policy over the following decades but suggested the somewhat extraordinary proposition that "Growth has no set limits in terms of population or resource use beyond which lies ecological disaster". (7)

The rationale for this proposition was that different limits obtain for the use of energy, raw materials, land and water, and that these will be made manifest in the form of rising costs and diminishing returns rather than any sudden disappearance of the resource base. Instead the development of technology and the accummulation of knowledge would in fact result in the enhancement of the carrying capacity of the resource base. It then advanced a number of conditions or "strategic imperatives for sustainable development"including the need for sufficient levels of growth to meet peoples' needs and aspirations without compromising the needs of future generations; the need for that growth to be more equitably shared both between and within nations; and the democratic participation of the world's people in decision making.

While the concept of "sustainable development" is still open to a number of interpretations and criticism, the debate has now moved on from the simple "growth versus development" arguments that began with Malthus, to include a concept of "growth" that is compatible with the idea of an improving standard of living for the world's people which is measured in terms of **quality of life** as much as in material terms, and which is environmentally sustainable.

Meanwhile the *Bruntland Report* was itself the subject of criticism and, because of differing interpretations of what is meant by development, the "growth versus environment" argument is still made by some people even in the context of sustainability.

THE NATURE AND SCALE OF THE PROBLEM

So what is the nature of this global environmental problem, which is now almost universally accepted as being able to be addressed only within the context of a new approach to what constitutes growth ?

We noted earlier, in the work referred to by Angus Maddison (*Phases of Capitalist Development*), that economic growth had been hardly measureable until the early years of the Industrial Revolution. Between 500 and 1500 European Gross Domestic Product (GDP) had grown at on average at a rate of some 0.1 per cent; between 1500 and 1700 at 0.3 per cent; between 1700 and 1820 at 0.6 per cent and then during the period 1820 to 1980 at 2.5 per cent. Ormerod noted that the growth rate in the earliest of these periods implied "that in 1500 the volume of economic activity in the West was between 2.5 and 3 times as great as it had been in 500... (and)... the Western economies grew as much in

percentage terms between 1950 and 1970 as they did between 500 and 1500...
And given the much higher base at the start of the 1950s the absolute increase in
volume of goods and services was enormously greater". (8)

Both the pace of growth and its impact on our Earth have continued to
accelerate on "history's fastest growth track" so that during the 20th century "the
world's population has multiplied more than three times; its economy has grown
twentyfold; the consumption of fossil fuels has grown by a factor of 30 and
industrial production by a factor of 50. **Most of that growth, about four fifths
of it, ocurred since 1950.**" (9) (emphasis added)

The product of this accelerating growth alas, has not been just a huge increase
in goods and services represented by growing levels of GDP, but a planet which
is increasingly unfit to live in.

WORLD POPULATION GROWTH

In 1972 when the MIT team published their *Limits to Growth* report they noted
that "in 1650 the population numbered about 0.5 billion (500 million) and it was
growing at a rate of approximately 0.3 per cent per year... (which)... corresponds
to a doubling time of nearly 250 years". (10) By 1970 the world's population had
grown to 3.6 billion and the rate of growth was then 2.1 per cent per year,
implying a doubling time of just 33.3 years.

In their second report *Beyond the Limits* published in 1992, they
acknowledged that because between 1971 and 1991 "death rates continued to
fall... [and]... birth rates on average fell slightly faster, there had been a
corresponding reduction in population growth rates... (but it was also true
that)... in 1991 there were still more people added to the world than in any year
ever before". (11)

The world population in fact stood at about 5.3 billion in 1991, and in just
another 30 years, i.e. in 2025 it is estimated that it will have grown to some 8.5
billion.

Of that additional 3.2 billion, "3 billion will be in the Third World countries
where millions already live on the edge of survival, on marginal and
unsustainable land". (12)

The implications of this exponential rise in the world's population for land,
food production and harvesting, energy, water, pressure on the rest of the
world's raw materials and exacerbation of global pollution problems, are clearly
very serious.

GREENHOUSE GASES

Perhaps the most widely discussed symptoms of this global environmental crisis
are the "Depletion of the Ozone Layer" and "Global Warming" which are a
reflection of, or feed-back from, environmental stresses deriving in large measure
from human economic activity.

The ozone layer in the atmosphere which protects us from the sun's harmful
ultraviolet rays is under attack from a number of gases released by plants, animals
and by humans. Chief amongst these are the Chloroflourocarbons (CFCs), very

widely used by industry and the general public in refrigerants, aerosols, foam blowing agents and solvents etc.

Other important greenhouse gases however include carbon dioxide(from burning fossil fuels and the loss of forest cover), methane (which rises from wetlands, from the digestive processes of livestock and humans, and from burning fossil fuels), and nitrous oxide (from fertilisers and again from the loss of forests and the burning of fossil fuels).

Together these gases are destroying the ozone layer and supplementing the natural heat trapping processes in the atmosphere, with the effect of increasing the risk of cancers in humans and a potentially dangerous rise in global temperature.

CLIMATE CHANGE

In a widely quoted report for the Intergovernmental Panel on Climate Change (IPCC) by R. A. Houghton et al., it is noted that while temperature and levels of greenhouse gases have previously changed together, without any specific cause being established, "current atmospheric concentrations of carbon dioxide and methane are far higher than they have been for 160,000 years".

The IPCC, also quoted by MacNeill et al. (13) in *Beyond Interdependence*, suggested that "If no steps are taken to limit greenhouse gas emissions, that is, if we continue with "business as usual", global mean temperatures will increase between 2.6 and 5.8 degrees Celsius over the next century".

The most significant effect of such higher temperatures is expected to be a rise in sea levels and IPCC estimate that over the next century sea levels are likely to rise between 30 and 100 centimetres, or up to one metre.

A further result is that some parts of the world would have increased rainfall while others, most notably the productive croplands of the Northern Hemisphere, might get a great deal less. As a consequence, although some regions may benefit, the global incidence of storms, flooding and drought would increase significantly.

Because of these changing climate patterns and poor land management, some 15 million acres of new desert are being created each year, while in both developed and developing countries huge swathes of fertile soil are being lost to flooding, drought and poor management.

Robert Allen's *How to Save the World* notes, for example, that "An area twice the size of Canada – 20 million square kilometers (nearly 8 million square miles) – is now on the brink of being turned into a desert" and goes on to record that "in the century in which it has been cultivated, southern Iowa (USA) has lost as much as half its top soil... [and]... if present rates of land impoverishment are allowed to persist, one third of the world's cropland will disappear in a mere 20 years". (14)

FORESTS

These problems of climate instability, induced by rising levels of greenhouse gases, and associated desertification and soil erosion, are further aggravated by the devastating loss of the great forests of the world. As Third World and other countries strive for economic growth, expanding exports and relief from crippling debt, so their tropical rainforests and northern coniferous forests (as well as many of the animal and other species which depend on them) are disappearing at an alarming rate.

In a World Resources Institute report in 1990, quoted in *The DEBT BOOMERANG*, it is suggested that recent studies relating to a number of key countries point to levels of deforestation in the tropics that may be a lot worse than was previously thought. Whereas it had been thought that until quite recently annual deforestation in the tropics was some 11.4 million hectares per annum the new studies point to an annual loss worldwide of "up to 20.4 million hectares (51 million acres) of tropical forest annually". (15)

As these enormous areas of tropical and coniferous forest are felled, burned and bulldozed each year, so huge amounts of carbon dioxide are added to the atmosphere every year and dozens of species are lost every day.

When we add the many alternative forms of air, chemical and toxic waste pollution, increasing water and energy shortage, the loss of fish stocks and other aquatic life, melting ice caps, increasing flows of economic refugees and many other manifestations of our over-exploitation of the earth, the prospects for increasing conflict and system breakdown can hardly be denied.

THE GROWTH DILEMMA

As we noted earlier, politicians and those whose guidance they ultimately follow continue to talk of "sustainable growth" or "sustainable development" with the implicit inclusion of global economic growth as an essential element. That they should continue to do so, in the face of such overwhelming evidence that growth is at the heart of the global environmental problem, is a mystery to many.

Perhaps Professor Slessor identifies at least part of the answer, when after noting the existence of an "industrial imperative" he quotes from the Conservation Society that, "Even those who do look a little further ahead are usually content to excuse their inaction by accepting the claims of the technological optimists"... [and]... "When, as in 1971, there is massive and growing unemployment, there is no obvious and immediate solution to the problems of gaining a livelihood except to generate expansion of the economy. All political parties, every Trade Unionist, each small businessman sees it as a device for his own immediate salvation... practically every voter votes with himself in mind, and votes for expansion. Live now, pay later". (16)

Certainly in a world where it is almost universally accepted that total population is on track to rise from some 5.5 billion in 1990 to around 10 billion by 2040, it is clear that there will be a resulting need for huge increases in food and other production.

J. MacNeill suggests in this context, that "if current forms of development were employed, a further five to tenfold boost in economic activity would be required over the next fifty years to meet the needs and aspirations of 10 billion people... [reflecting]... the continuance of annual growth rates of 3.2 to 4.7 per cent". (17)

And politicians in turn feel they simply cannot offer the prospects of annual growth rates that are much less than those and still expect to be elected.

It is surely not unreasonable that they should indeed advocate such levels of growth in the Third World. By increasing per capita incomes there such growth could, at least for a while, actually be good for the environment. It is widely recognised for example, that acute poverty often results in an increasing population as families try to ensure that there are more hands to contribute income and to provide security for parental old age. With some reasonable economic growth and/or more equitable distribution of national product, the pressure to produce large families will almost certainly be relieved, and the pressures on the carrying capacity of the land, water and forest may be similarly reduced.

It is a vastly different matter however in the developed world. In the industrial countries 20 per cent of the world's population already consume 75 per cent of the world's goods and services. The average European or North American consumer uses up to "almost 16 times as much of the world's food, energy and material resources as his counterpart in the Third World countries". (18)

Continued annual growth rates of 3 to 5 per cent in the already industrialised countries therefore, simply cannot be sustained without further devastating impact on the global environment and increased tension between these countries and those of the Third World.

Yet even in the industrialised countries, despite continuing growth, the gap between the incomes of the rich and those of the poor is continuously widening. Any promise therefore by a political party to deliver zero or very low growth, even in the interests of the global environment or the peoples of the Third World, would almost certainly ensure electoral defeat.

And if it were thought just possible that curtailment of growth in the industrialised countries might be acceptable to their electorates if accommpanied by re-distribution of income designed to close the gap between rich and poor, it certainly would be unacceptable to those who control the international financial system.

They are the final arbiters in economic decision making and they rely on continuous growth for survival of the system. It is in their interests therefore that politicians and other opinion formers, as well as voters, continue to advocate economic growth despite the environmental consequences.

The world's peoples therefore are in a dangerous and pressing environmental Catch 22 situation which needs to be urgently resolved.

On the one hand, the financial system that drives economic activity cannot survive without continuous growth. At the same time growth, at least for some years, represents the only hope that the huge majority of the world's population have for a decent standard of living.

On the other hand the prospect now seems real that if this imperative to economic growth (and to escalating national and international debt) is allowed to continue unrestrained, we must soon face a breakdown of the global environment so severe, that it will put in jeopardy the human life support system.

Notes
1. Rio Declaration   1992 Annex 1
2. Boulding K. E.   1992 p. 27/35
3. Mishan E. J.   1969 p. 62/64
4. Meadows D. H. et al.   1974 p. 23/24
5. Meadows D. H. et al.   1992 p. xiii (preface)
6. Meadows D. H. et al.   1992 p. xiii
7. World Commission on Environment
    and Development   1987 p. 45
8. Ormerod P.   1994 p. 10
9. MacNeill J. et al.   1991 p. 3/5
10. Meadows D. H. et al.   1974 p. 34
11. Meadows D. H. et al.   1992 p. 24
12. Porritt J.   1990 p. 17
13. MacNeill J. et al.   1991 p. 13
14. Allen R.   1992 p. 12
15. George S.   1992 p. 9
16. Slessor M.   1972 p. 120
17. MacNeill J. et al.   1991 p. 5
18. Todaro M. P.   1989 p. 203

CHAPTER
4

UNEMPLOYMENT

Unemployment is one of the most important problems that policy makers face in virtually all of the industrial and developing countries of the world.

It is the issue which is usually centre stage in the economic debate and there is as yet no consensus on its causes or how it might be eliminated. And certainly nowhere in the mainstream of political or economic discussion is it remotely accepted that "unemployment", even in the form of desirable leisure, might in fact be an attractive economic and social objective.

Yet there is a slowly growing, albeit reluctant recognition that the traditional economic policy goal of "full employment" may just already be impossible of achievement on any sustainable basis.

CATEGORIES OF UNEMPLOYMENT

Economists traditionally identify, within the global figures, a number of kinds and causes of unemployment including:-

Seasonal unemployment which affects those who work in industries affected by weather or other seasonal factors, e.g. building, agriculture and tourism.

Frictional unemployment which involves those who are entering the workforce for the first time, are re-entering after absence, for example to rear a family, and those who are between jobs.

Structural unemployment which is essentially a mis-match between vacancies and available skills, or vacancies and available labour.

Cyclical unemployment which rises and falls with the cycle of economic activity and which, when the cycle turns down every few years, has traditionally been seen as being by far the greatest component of total unemployment.

They then develop a range of theories that try to explain in more detail the nature of these unemployment types, and offer some proposals for their remedy.

Technological unemployment however has recently become a major concern and there is as yet little by way of prescription for its resolution beyond the structural need for increased levels of labour skills, training and development to help mitigate labour market imperfections and match the pace of technological change.

What follows in this chapter therefore, is a short discussion on the economic cycle and its related cyclical unemployment, and then a more comprehensive consideration of technological unemployment which now threatens to make a major contribution to final failure of the current financial/economic system.

UNEMPLOYMENT AND ECONOMIC CYCLES

That total levels of unemployment rise and fall with economic cycles is universally recognised. There is less consensus however on what causes, and therefore what remedy might be applied to mitigate the impact of, these cycles.

The phenomenon of economic cycles has been noted and subjected to analysis, since at least 1865 when the work of Clement Juglar was published. Richardson and Snyder (1) in the introduction to their translation of Kondratief's papers which they entitle *The Long Wave Cycle*, note that while Schumpeter in 1939 "identified a 3-4 year business cycle and a longer 10 year Jugler cycle", Kondratief had in 1922/28 identified much longer economic cycles or waves, with some 54 years between their peaks and troughs.

They go on to confirm how their own studies, and historical data compiled by Warren and Pearson, show "unmistakeably that there was a long wave in a roughly 50 year cycle pattern in economics... [and that]... a 54 year cycle can be found in the history of agriculture prices going back to 1260".

In support of this position, they subsequently quote from a speech by Professor Forrester of the Massachusetts Institute of Technology(MIT), where he says in explanation of these long waves, "We are coming to believe that there is little effect on business cycles from interest rates, credit availability and investment tax incentives. The time intervals involved in Capital construction are too long to fit within the short span of a business cycle... The wearing out of Capital plant takes 15 to 40 years... [and]... Such long periods of time are not compatible with a business cycle that comes along and goes about every four years... In fact variations in Capital Investment participate directly in the two longer cycles of economic fluctuations – the 15 to 25 year Kuznets cycle, and the 45 to 60 year long wave". His proposition is that "The long wave involves an overbuilding of the Capital sector in which it grows beyond the capital output rate needed for long term equilibrium. Capital plant throughout an economy is overbuilt beyond the level justified by the marginal productivity of Capital... [and]... Finally over-expansion is ended by the hiatus of a great depression during which excess Capital plant is physically worn out and is financially depreciated on the account books until the economic stage has been cleared for a new era of re-building."

While there **is** clearly an underlying economic cyclical "long wave", and we might accept that major items of Capital can take some 15 to 40 years to wear out, Professor Forrester's proposition is surely incomplete. It is hardly likely after all, that throughout the industrial world the dates of acquisition and life-end of myriad Capital items actually coincide by simple chance, closely enough to be the principal cause of regular periodic collapse of the international economic system. If they do coincide in this way so as to be a major causal factor in periodic depressions, there must surely be some deeper underlying explanation for such **systematic** behaviour.

It is the contention here that, the critical factor directly inducing both the short business cycle and the longer Kuznets and Kondratief type cycles, with their related "cyclical unemployment", is not in fact the overbuilding and subsequent working out of Capital per se. Nor is it the rise and fall of "investor confidence" that Keynes insisted upon and which undoubtedly does occur. It is rather the nature and operation of the debt-money system which is the root cause of the short and long economic cycles.

Recall from Chapter One, how during the expansionary phase of the business cycle there is a gathering shortfall in the distribution of consumer purchasing power relative to prices, because prices must include both profit and interest payments for which no money has been put into circulation in the **same time period**. There is a resulting rise in levels of undistributed goods and services, and of debt. Banks then begin to fear widespread bankruptcies and debt repudiation. Overdraft facilities are withdrawn, private sector loans are called in and simultaneously pressure is put on governments to reduce their borrowing requirements by reducing public expenditure and/or increasing taxation. The deflationary period of the business cycle follows and is accompanied by rising levels of unemployment.

In due course, as surpluses are **partially dispersed** (by consumption, export, sale below cost or waste), the rising price level that characterised the boom phase is temporarily restrained. It is now vital for the banks, that a new expansionary phase should get under way and they follow aggressive lending policies to ensure that it does. Traditionally this has led to employment levels rising again towards the prospect of "full employment" until, within a few years, the deflationary phase recurs and unemployment rises again.

There is however, during the "long wave" that underlies these short business cycles, a rising **trend in accruing surpluses and total debt**. The result is periodically much more severe phases of deflation in which all the characteristics of the down-turn in the short business cycle are greatly magnified. These periods are now referred to as "depressions".

As they occur, with increasing severity, they bring with them not just severe deflation, but a heightened threat to the survival of the financial system.

The reaction of the banking fraternity is therefore correspondingly more robust, and the impact on economic activity, employment and the general welfare of society is even more painful.

There has of course always been periodic short term relief from cyclical unemployment and related problems as bust gave way to boom in the short business cycle, and as the destruction of war finally cleared the way for "recovery" from greater depressions. To extend this relief so that it continues over the long term, economists and governments have sought to help "stabilise" fluctuations in employment levels by the general application of Keynesian and then Monetarist policies and by developing a range of more specific theories (Job Search, Insider/Outsider, Implicit Contracts, Efficiency Wage etc.) designed to explain and provide remedies for the perceived inherent imperfections of the labour market. None however has, or can, succeed so long as the current debt-money system continues to drive economic activity.

Meanwhile, it is becoming more widely recognised that of even greater significance than cyclical unemployment is the impact of accelerating technological change. Its effect is to ensure an underlying and irreversible rising trend in unemployment which is only marginally affected by the cycle of economic activity and from which, short of war, there can be no lasting respite.

TECHNOLOGY AND UNEMPLOYMENT

The natural tendency to technological innovation is increasingly being stimulated by the need to reduce input costs, especially those of labour. This relentless drive to reduce costs reflects the need for ever greater profit levels from which to maintain dividends to shareholders, while meeting escalating debt service payments to banks. This point is underlined by the observation of Maddison when he notes that "A major driving force of modern economies is the strong propensity to risk capital on new techniques that hold the promise of improving profits, in stark contrast to the defensive wariness of the pre-capitalist approach to technology". (2)

An example from America of the sheer scale of the pressure in this process is given by Hixson (3) when he shows how the **income** of Proprietorships and Partnerships, **before payment of interest**, rose from $36 billion in 1947 to $401.9 billion in 1987 – a growth multiple of 11.1. Yet over the same period the amount they had to **pay in interest alone**, rose from $0.8 billion to $89 billion, a growth multiple of 111.3!

The resulting modern technological "revolution" may indeed be delivering reduced costs and allowing business operations temporarily to stay ahead of rising debt service costs. But it is also the major cause of the rising international trend in unemployment, as men and women are relaced by "machines".

It is ironic therefore, that while technological change is partly driven by pursuit of higher profits from which to repay bank loans and related interest, it simultaneously ensures irreversible mass unemployment and the associated loss of purchasing power, that puts the banking system at even greater risk of collapse.

A short review of the nature of technological change; its enormous impact on productivity; the pace at which it continues to accelerate, and its impact on consumer purchasing power through loss of paid employment, will help to demonstrate why it represents such a threat to any hope of long term full employment for wages or salaries and to the finance/economic system.

BACKGROUND

In line with "God's curse" upon Adam that, "In the sweat of thy face shalt thou eat bread", the great mass of men and women have gained access to a share of the world's wealth only as a reward for work. So for many thousands of years men and women spent their days hunting and gathering food. Always though they had a little energy left to provide the basis of progress – the invention of increasingly sophisticated weapons and tools, which in turn allowed a further increase in surplus energy and time for other purposes including creative activity. Man-made tools and machines, ideas, information and organisational expertise were handed on from generation to generation creating a "common cultural inheritance".

This inheritance has been hugely expanded, at an accelerating pace, as we have increasingly resorted to the division of labour, given priority to the sciences in education, found more efficient methods of tapping solar energy, and dramatically improved the nature, range and power of our tools, machines, computers and our approach to organisation. The result has been, especially over the last 100 to 150 years, a dramatic and continuing reduction in our need to work for our survival.

Indeed although there are probably more people working today than ever before, it would have to be widely acknowledged that much of the work done now is in fact make-work designed simply to maintain paid employment (for example in the production of military equipment which is unnecessary for domestic defence and unrelated to any conflict involving the manufacturing country), or is related to leisure activites such as sport and travel which are not **materially** productive.

At the same time as the technological revolution accelerates, we note rapidly increasing numbers who seek jobs but are unemployed, while simultaneously enormous surpluses and great waste continue to be manifest in the industrial countries.

Certainly in the past, as unemployment resulted from the introduction of new technology in one sector of the economy there was a corresponding expansion of employment in some other, often new sector, although usually with a significant time lag that brought pain to those made unemployed by the initial impact of the new technology.

Yet the pace of technological change (surely incontrovertibly the most powerful influence in modern economic growth), continues to accelerate at bewildering speed. And as we enter the era of micro-technology and artificial intelligence applied to robots, it offers the prospect that we might satisfy all our material needs with an even more rapidly diminishing human input in the form of wage related work. It is almost certainly possible even now to lift the "Curse of Adam".

In any case there is certainly less room for confidence that alternative demands for labour will continue to ensure that all who want paid work may find it. Indeed as the last chapter suggested it seems certain that, quite apart from technological considerations, environmental constraints will ensure significant limits to growth and therefore to any expansion of paid employment.

This potential for a dramatic decline in opportunities for paid employment is critically important to the current economic system because paid work is vital to the "successful" operation of the economy today. It is the mechanism through which by far the greatest proportion of consumer purchasing power, in the form of wages and salaries, is distributed within the economy.

If the new technological revolution does greatly diminish the need for labour input to the production process, then it will no longer be possible to regard wages and salaries as an effective method of distributing goods and services produced in a market economy. Indeed it has been suggested that if we were to exploit fully the potential of the existing industrial system, unemployment would already be unmanageable.

TECHNOLOGY AND GROWTH

Developments in technology – from the discovery of fire to the invention of the wheel and on to the development of navigational aids and the harnessing of steam – have always been the catalyst that triggered further acceleration in economic growth and social progress.

With the great discoveries and inventions that provided the launch pad for the industrial revolution, this relevance of technical change to economic growth was increasingly acknowledged by observers and students of socio-economic development.

In fact the consequences of technical change represented by scientific discoveries like the existence of "latent heat" by Joseph Black (giving the clue to the enormous energy content of steam) and its exploitation in due course in James Watt's steam engine; the use of gas by Murdoch as the source of industrial and municipal lighting, and Clerk-Maxwell's epoch making work on electro-magnetism which led to radio, radar and a flood of other revolutionary technical achievements, could hardly fail to be noted by entrepreneurs and economic historians. But while their reaction was to accept that this explosion of technology had a major impact on economic activity and growth, at the same time they failed to consider in any comprehensive way how these effects of technical change should be explained in either concrete or technical terms.

Their problem in this context reflected a general view that technical change was somehow different from pure science which was concerned with understanding the nature of the universe, and the result very often was a long delay between scientific discovery and its practical application to economic activity. Maxwell's theory of electro-magnetism for example was developed in 1860, yet it was towards the end of the century before Marconi established a commercial company to apply these discoveries to the development of radio.

However as the engineering profession grew and there was a rapid expansion of industrial and government research, so there was a quite new conjunction of science and technology. This in turn increased greatly the speed with which new discoveries were applied to the economic process.

But the difficulties in accurately explaining the role of technology in economic growth continued, partly because technology was thought of as somehow operating outwith the economic system and because there were problems in applying a clear definition to the nature of technology.

Even in 1969 for example, it was suggested that... "it may be thought of as Society's pool of knowledge related to the principles of physical and social phenomena (properties of fluids and laws of motion) or knowledge related to the day to day operations of production". (4)

Technological change then might be seen as an advance that introduced new methods of producing existing products, innovation in the development of new products or new techniques of marketing or organisation. It might affect current production or lead to change over time. Almost inevitably however any attempt to try to explain its relationship to economic growth tended to be complex.

For all these reasons it was **only in the post World War II period that economic analysis began to emphasise the importance of technological**

change as the major source of economic growth.

In 1957, a very influential piece of analysis by R. M. Solow under the title *Technical Progress and Productivity Change*, stimulated new interest in the issue. He presented in that year his estimates for the relative contribution made to economic growth by capital accummulation and technical progress in the USA from 1909 to 1949. These suggested that of total growth in productivity per man hour, only 0.125 could be attributed to capital accummulation, with the "residual" of 0.875 (defined as technical change) being due to shifts in the production function as a consequence of technological progress.

His work was much criticised, and although Solow subsequently accepted much of the criticism, his paper is still considered to be a classic in its field. Solow's later work relaxed major assumptions to allow that technical progress was "embodied" in capital and then capital accummulation – acting as a vehicle for technical progress – itself became much more significant in explaining growth.

In the middle 1960s Simon Kuznets (5) in his *Modern Economic Growth* described the economic growth of nations "as a sustained increase in per capita output (or per worker product) usually accompanied by... sweeping structural change". He suggested that it was helpful to consider this process over long spans of time which might be distinguished as distinct "epochs of growth", in which long periods of change begin with a critical technological breakthrough leading in turn to an enormous change in the "pool of knowledge". He went on to illustrate that for all countries, this process of technological change and economic growth, was without exception **"accommpanied by a significant long term decline in man hours per capita output"**. (emphasis added)

By 1969 E. Mansfield was also convinced and felt able to claim in his *Economies of Technical Change*, that "without doubt technical change is one of the most important determinants of the shape and evolution of the US economy... which led to... an increased range and flow of products and **allowed a reduction of working hours**". (6) (emphasis added)

The impact of technical change on production can be different of course in different circumstances. For example, if the rate of output for a given product and the relative prices for both capital and labour are held constant, technical change will have a neutral effect if it results in the same per cent reduction of both capital and labour. If however it results in a greater reduction in capital required it will be capital saving, and if the reverse is true it will of course be labour saving.

However technical change that might be thought capital saving (e.g. Watt's steam engine as it precipitated the retirement of many work horses and instead increased job opportunities for the men who now made, operated and serviced the machines that replaced them), often also developes to become labour saving.

Computers are a good case in point. They can operate many orders of magnitude faster than mechanical machinery and they do not wear out in the normal sense. The first computers were physically huge and very expensive, so that their immediate impact tended to be capital saving – as they replaced or enhanced major items of plant and machinery.

However with the development of micro-electronics, not only was there the prospect of rising output with a significant reduction in the total inputs of energy, capital and labour thus making it possible to "maximise two advantages – high output and low input at once" (7), there was also a dramatic fall in computer prices. As this process of miniaturisation and falling cost has continued there has been an almost exponential increase in their labour saving application in factories, offices and shops.

As further development of computer technology leads to the application of artificial intelligence to industrial robots, this potential for labour saving is magnified many times.

Indeed a glimpse of this potential may be had from the experience of the industrialised countries in time of war. During the second World War for example, the standard of living in the USA is reported to have risen by 40 per cent despite having 21 million people engaged in the armed forces or in arms production and large resources allocated to research into atomic energy. (8)

Bertrand Russell's view that the British experience closely paralled that of the USA was made clear in his essay *In Praise of Idleness*, where he commented that "World War II showed conclusively that, by scientific organisation, it is possible to keep modern populations in fair comfort on a small part of the working capacity of the modern world. If at the end of the war, the scientific organisation which had been created in order to liberate men and women for fighting and munitions work had been preserved, and working hours cut to four, all would have been well. Instead of that the old chaos was restored, those whose work was demanded were made to work long hours, and the rest were left to starve as unemployed".

And today, as the pace of technological change accelerates at bewildering speed without any corresponding re-organisation of social arrangements that might ensure the equitable distribution of the resulting abundance, we find in fact that "unemployment tends to be in inverse proportion to demand". (9)

Barry Jones illustrates this contention by a list of some twenty examples which include:

US Agriculture is the most abundant in world history but its share of the labour force has fallen dramatically from 38 per cent in 1900 to 3% in 1978.

Japan, with large production runs and high technology, produces an average of 94 cars per worker per annum – but Toyota, the largest producer, has a far lower labour content than Mazda. The Nissan factory has an assembly line two kilometers long, in which work is 97 per cent automated and 3,200 workers produce 420,000 vehicles per annum, an average of 131.25 per worker. In the Australian motor industry 360,000 units are manufactured by 80,000 production workers, an annual average of 4.5 units per worker. If Australia increased its production runs to compete on world markets these existing ratios could not be maintained.

Production of colour television sets in Japan increased from 8.4 million in 1972 to 10.5 million in 1976 (an increase of 25%) while the number of employees making them fell from 47,886 to 25,667 (a decrease of 46%). Phillips, the world's largest electrical manufacturing company estimated that even after allowing for a 3% real increase in annual turnover, by 1990 it would be over-manned by 56%.

How then can we begin to square this evidence with the still strongly expressed view of many politicians, economists and the general public, that increases in the rate of technological change will not necessarily result in increasing aggregate unemployment?

Such a view usually reflects a continuing belief or hope that, while technological change may indeed be the major determinant of increased productivity and economic growth, any resulting loss of employment in one sector of the economy will still in time be fully compensated for by the emergence of new industries with the subsequent restoration of a "natural rate" of full employment.

A closer examination of historical experience, both general and industry specific, and of forecasts for further changes in technology might help determine whether this view can be justified.

THE BIG PICTURE

THE UK

If we look at some UK statistical data which refer to the general economy during the period from the early 1960s to the early 1990s, a picture emerges which is broadly similar across the major industrial countries.

Over the period 1972 to 1993, the UK population grew by some 3. 9% from a total of 55.812 million to 57.649 million, with roughly similar growth in respect of both sexes. The economically active sector(the total employed plus those in the workforce but unemployed) also grew by some 12.2% in the same period, although some care is needed when interpreting these figures because of differential growth in male compared to female economic activity. (10) Output in the UK however grew much faster and the index of Gross Domestic Product (at 1990 market prices) grew as in Table 3, reflecting a substantial growth in output over the period.

TABLE 3: Gross Domestic Product (Source:CSO Blue Book 1995: Table 1. 1)					
1973	1978	1983	1988	1990	1994
72.3	75.2	80.9	97.9	100	105.8

These are quite impressive increases in output when they are considered against a much slower growth in the economically active population. It would be hard to deny that to a large extent, they reflect the embodiment of technical advances in productive capital.

We noted earlier that access to a share of that increasing National Income is overwhelmingly through paid employment. To do no more than maintain the prevailing pattern of income distribution therefore, broadly requires that any displacement of workers by technology in one industry should be fully compensated by the development of new industries and associated new job opportunities.

Certainly this has largely been the historical experience. As technology has been applied to the development of new techniques and mechanisation in agriculture for example, there have been large increases in productivity and a corresponding fall in the number of agricultural workers employed. But parallel with these changes, if not quite synchronised with them, there was a great expansion in manufacturing.

Similarly, as manufacturing industry increasingly applied capital embodied technology and new techniques, the process was repeated and service industries grew to compensate for falling employment in manufacturing.

The process has been in train since the beginning of the industrial revolution some 200 years ago and Tables 4 and 5 illustrate that it continues at an accelerating pace.

TABLE 4: GROSS DOMESTIC PRODUCT AT CONSTANT FACTOR COSTS: by industry of output. Source: CSO Blue Book 1992, Table 2. 4				
	1981	1985	1989	1991
Agriculture	85.2	100	101	109.1
Manufacturing (Total)	91	100	119	112. 2
Services:				
a. Distribution, Catering etc.	86	100	123.3	118.3
b. Transport, Communications etc.	89.9	100	125.6	123.9
c. Banks, Insurance etc.	76	100	138	138
d. Public Admin, Defence, Social Services	102	100	98	101
e. Education & Health	96	100	108	108

TABLE 5: PERSONS EMPLOYED IN UK ('000s) (Source CSO Blue Books, 1984 Table 1. 17, 1995 Table 7. 17: Social Trends 1970 Table 26. * incl. mining & quarrying)				
	1961	1973	1980	1991
Agriculture	1324*	432	361	287
Manufacturing	8794	7861	6939	4708
Construction	1478	1320	1252	990
Services:				
a. Distribution, Catering etc.	3361	3950	4318	4757
b. Transport, Communication etc.	1702	1507	1483	1350
c. Banks and Insurance etc.	556	1442	1714	2763
d. Education, Health, Pub. Admin., Defence & Social Services	3437	4445	4976	4922
Services Total	9056	11344	12491	13792
Overall Total	20652	20957	21043	19777

At first reading, these figures suggest that despite large gains in labour productivity resulting in considerable displacement of labour as industries have matured, employment in services had to a large extent, though by no means fully, compensated for these losses. It might be thought reasonable therefore that this process could be expected to continue as the normal outcome of technical and economic progress. There is no doubt that many economists and others do in fact still take this view.

However there are powerful indications which suggest that such optimism should be attended by some reservation. For example, despite the fact that there has been an increase in total numbers employed, there has been also a significant rising trend in unemployment.

TABLE 6: General Levels of Unemployment % in UK (Source ILO Year Books)									
1965	1975	1976	1978	1979	1980	1981	1982	1983	1984
1.5	4.0	5.5	5.8	5.7	6.8	10.4	10.9	11.7	11.6
1985	1986	1987	1988	1989	1990	1991	1992	1993	
11.8	11.8	10.6	8.4	6.3	5.9	8.1	8.9	10.4	

Throughout the period 1957 to 1970 unemployment never rose above 2. 4%. But since then the trend has been inexorably upwards, with levels again in 1995 at about 10%, after a modest respite of some three or four years from the prolonged high levels of the 1980s.

EUROPE

The European Commissioner for social affairs, Vasso Papandreo, was reported in the *Scotsman* newspaper of July 23rd 1992 as having introduced the EC Annual Report with a forecast that in 1992 the EC rate of unemployment will increase to between 9.5% and 9.7% in 1993.

Because these figures represent a European average it was thought that unemployment in some countries, including the UK, would continue above 10% for the foreseeable future. A similar forecast by the OECD countries was also reported as suggesting that even if economic growth were some 3% in 1993, this would hardly affect unemployment – the expectation being that total unemployment might fall from 29.9 million in 1992 to 29.4 million in 1993.

In 1995, the London *Times* reporting in its edition of May 24th on a new OECD announcement, noted that "In its latest jobs study, the OECD... said yesterday that although unemployment is now edging down from its peak, policymakers will still have to "confront a major problem of high and persistent unemployment... [and]... unemployment looks set to remain high even when the cyclical recovery is complete".

At the same time, when we consider again the UK position, it is clear that despite the growth in the economically active sector of the population between 1972 and 1993, that growth has not been balanced between the sexes. It reflects in fact a drop from 63% to 57.9% in the economic activity rate of males and an increase in female economic activity from 32.6% to 42.3% in the same period (11). Since female employment is currently largely characterised by unskilled, often temporary work involving lower than average earnings and shorter hours, this differential trend in male and female activity rates distorts the employment figures and must also have the effect of reducing the total purchasing power distributed to consumers by way of wages and salaries for labour input.

The rapidly growing trend in short term "contract" employment and its associated insecurity may be expected to further aggravate this problem to a considerable extent.

Altogether it must be increasingly difficult to be optimistic that new sources of employment will indeed be created to the degree needed to compensate fully for the loss of employment currently being experienced in established industries. On the other hand, it may still be argued that we are simply observing that employment in mature sectors of the economy and compensating employment in the new sectors, like services and communications, are simply not synchronised and that in due course all will be well again. A look at what is happening in a couple of relevant industries might provide useful clues as to whether such optimism is likely to be justified.

MANUFACTURING INDUSTRY: MACHINE TOOLS

We have already noted that rapid changes in technology have dramatically increased productivity and have been accompanied by a large reduction in employment.

We can see more clearly how the process develops by looking at a specific division of industry within the manufacturing sector. The Machine Tool industry is especially useful to our discussion because it has always been a very important channel by which technology was introduced to general manufacturing, while it has itself experienced acutely the effects of that process.

This has been especially true as the introduction of Numeric Control (NC) and subsequently Computer Numeric Control (CNC), to the operation of machine tools in the mid 1970s, greatly increased their contribution to general productivity.

They were as a result much in demand by manufacturers and their share of the total machine tool production rose from 10% in 1978 to 39% in 1990.

FIG. 1: THE GROWTH OF NUMERIC CONTROLLED MACHINES (NC & CNC)
(Source: The Machine Tool Technology Association. Machine Tool Statistics 1991 – latest figs.)

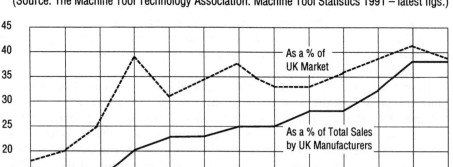

It is worth noting here that, while NC machine tools in 1990 show impressive growth to 39% of total machine tool production in the UK, the corresponding shares of total production in 1990 in Germany and Japan were 49% and 76% respectively.

Yet despite a fall in price as the new technologies became more common, total output of machine tools actually fell (because of their impact on general manufacturing productivity? – see Fig. 2) while the machine tool industry itself became more productive and reduced its labour force.

FIG. 2: UK MACHINE TOOL PRODUCTION & CONSUMPTION – 1968-1990
(Source: The Machine Tool Technology Association)

FIG. 3: QUARTERLY INDICES OF PRODUCTION & EMPLOYMENT 1984-1990 (1985 = 100)
(Source: The Machine Tool Technology Association)

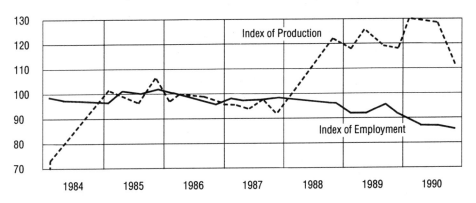

NB. Sections of the graph where the index of production line is above that for the index of employment show productivity was better than in the base year (1985) while the opposite is true where the lines are reversed.

Since NC machine tools began rapidly to increase their share of total output therefore, productivity in the machine tool industry has itself increased and employment has dropped unremittingly over the same period, from 35,700 in the first quarter of 1981 to 20,000 in the last quarter of 1990. (12)

There are no readily available long term forecasts for employment prospects in the industry, but forecasts of UK production in 1992 were for 10% growth in total consumption of machine tools (of which some may be imported) and a slightly higher increase in the NC/CNC machines' share of the total. (13)

Although the total production of machine tools in Germany and Japan is much larger than in the UK, we have noted already that the dominance of NC and CNC machines in their total outputs is even more marked.

The machine tool industry therefore demonstrates on an international basis, a clear causal link between technological development and growth in productivity and reducing levels of employment, which reverberates through the whole of the manufacturing sector.

We shall note later how this impact will be further increased as the introduction of robotic control and guidance accelerates over the next few years.

Meanwhile it was suggested earlier that, at least to a significant degree, fall out of labour from manufacturing might be compensated for by increasing job opportunities especially in the service sector. A review of one of the most important of the service sector "industries" may be useful in testing this proposition.

BANKING AND INSURANCE

We saw that up to 1991 this expectation was largely fulfilled and in fact in one of the most important industries in the service sector – Banking, Insurance etc. – there was a very rapid and impressive increase in employment from 556,000 in 1961 to 2,763,000 in 1991!

But the service industries it seems are not immune from the impact of technology on employment any more than manufacturing and other sectors have been. Banking and Insurance for example, has been subject to enormous levels of investment in new technology since the late 1970s.

Concentration has been on the introduction of "Cash Machines" (ATM's), regional processing centres, and communications systems. By 1991 banks alone had 16,000 of these cash machines handling £33 billion, up some 2,000% since 1980. (14)

But Sir John Quinton of Barclay's Bank is quoted (15) as confirming that "every cash machine eliminated half a human teller" representing 8,000 jobs to 1991.

Massive investment in the development of regional processing centres and communications systems have resulted in even greater job losses as the need for secretarial and other skills diminishes and large parts of the branch networks are closed. Some 2,842 bank and building society branches for example, were lost between 1990 and 1993. The Bank, Insurance and Financial Services Union (BIFU) literature highlights quotes from bank managements to confirm that these job losses have been deliberately planned as the fruit of investment in technology.

Brian Pearce, Chief Executive of Midland Bank is reported in the *Independent* newspaper of February 28th 1992 as proposing that "the number of bank and building society branches in Britain should be halved from the present 20,000", while Brian Pitman, Chief Executive of Lloyds is quoted, in referring to a new £17 million automated system that, "each of the 700 new machines do the work of four people processing cheques and credit slips" and in the *Independent* of February 22nd 1992, he confirms that "an efficiency drive at Lloyds which cost 8,500 jobs last year could eliminate a further 2,000 or 3,000 in 1992, with more job cuts up to 1994 and beyond".

These reported job losses (or jobs at risk) are seen to be spread across the financial sector as in Table 7.

TABLE 7: JOB LOSSES(OR AT RISK) IN THE FINANCIAL SECTOR (Source: BIFU)				
	1990	1991	1992	TO 1995
Banking	11,819	22,406	21,970	16,800
Insurance		1,173	1,004	
Building Societies	66	315	15	
Finance Houses		1,033	775	
Other Financial Institutions	280	827	633	
T & S Staff	965	1,393	82	
Overall Total	13,130	27,147	24,479	
TOTAL 1990-1992			64,756	

From 1965 to 1990 we noted that it was Banking, Insurance etc. that had provided the major part of alternative jobs in the private services sector, to counter the fall out of job opportunities in other sectors, and especially in manufacturing.

Yet now, in the astonishly short period of twelve or so years, and because of the carefully planned introduction of new technology, this process has been reversed to the point where the "saviour" itself is losing tens of thousands of jobs each year and is expected to do so for some time to come. Indeed between 1990 and 1995 the "finance industry may well have lost more than 110, 000 jobs". (16) Meanwhile the process continues to accelerate as Building Societies convert to banks and merger follows merger in the financial sector.

This experience of the Machine Tool and the Banking and Insurance industries is especially interesting because now, in a way that was not the case in the 1950s and 1960s, it can be seen beyond dispute that these job losses are directly related to technological innovation. In fact we see it openly acknowledged by leading figures in Banking that the introduction of technology is specifically designed to have this effect.

On the face of it then, it would seem that virtually no area of economic activity is exempt from the impact of technological change on employment, which is then superimposed on, but quite independent of, "cyclical" unemployment. Therefore as this direct connection is clearly made between technology and unemployment, it becomes important to consider how the nature and accelerating pace of continuing technical change might continue to affect future levels of unemployment.

THE INFORMATION AND ROBOT REVOLUTION

While the impact of technology is currently manifest in almost every area of human activity, its effects are likely to be even more profound as the application of artificial intelligence to robots becomes more commonplace. We have noted that the development of the electronic computer and its application to the manufacturing process created a potential for economic change, even greater than that represented by the harnessing of steam power and electricity. Even early computers had qualitative differences when compared to other machines – they had the potential to operate at many orders of magnitude faster; were almost impervious to wearing out, and could process and store huge quantities of information. Those differences were further enhanced, at astonishing speed, by miniaturisation and falling prices so that by the mid-1970s they had become widespread in their application to manufacturing and many other sectors of the economy.

By 1980 progress was such that in Japan there was launched a "5th generation computer project", designed to incorporate artificial intelligence (AI) and "to produce a computer system with common sense which would be able to draw on related items from its knowledge base in making judgements concerning matters which it had been given no instructions about". (17)

The way would be open then for the application of intelligent computer control to industrial and other "robots" which had previously operated mechanically and routinely on the basis of relatively simple pre-programmed applications. Robots were to be able to make decisions on the basis of some understanding of the environment in which they were set to work.

As a result, a huge range of tasks "which could previously only be performed by highly trained human beings, including. . control of factory machinery" (18) would be expected fall to the robots.

These objectives were quickly met!

In the USA for example, after some early difficulties involving the failure of a number of robot suppliers, optimism was quickly revived. As early as 1985, Walter K Wiesel, President of the Robot Industry Association in the USA, in his address to the 15th International Symposium on Industrial Robots in Tokyo, was able to suggest that this renewed optimism reflected the fact that "re-programmable, multi-functional manipulators of today are more skilled than ever before. Advances in machine vision, tactile sensing and mobility are making robots suitable for tasks in an ever increasing range of industries. As robots learn to see, touch and move they gain increasing acceptance in industries such as automobiles, home appliances, aerospace, consumer goods, electronics, and off-road vehicles. Additionally, robots are making inroads in industries such as textiles, food processing, pharmaceuticals, furniture construction and health care". (19)

Other papers delivered to that symposium gave graphic illustration of the degree to which robots were already becoming capable of operations which just a year or two earlier were well beyond their ability. R. Svenson for example, in his paper *ASEA Robotics*, confirmed that "assembly of cars, includes many operations where parts like doors, fenders, wheels, windows etc., are currently mounted on the car bodies manually because of difficulty in measuring and adjusting the gap and flush between car parts and body... [but]... it was now possible with the new ASEA vision system in conjuction with ASEA robots to achieve accurate positioning automatically". (20)

H. W. Warnecke in another paper relating to wire harness assembly suggested that "up to now wiring harnesses (which are important components of many products including automobiles, household manufactures, office communications and space technology) have had to be made manually, but now the Frauhofer Institute for Manufacturing Engineering and Automation (IPA) in Stuttgart, has developed a variety of concepts for flexible automatic stations for wiring harness assembly, which allows economic assembly automation of small and large complex harnesses". (21)

It is clear therefore that the development of highly sophisticated and "inexpensive" robots, was already in 1985 offering the prospect of much deeper penetration into labour intensive industries. Even those jobs which had appeared secure because they involved human control and guidance of machines were now also under threat from robotisation.

Now in the 1990s, at the same time as the micro chip is subject to staggering increases in ability to store and manipulate information, it is being combined with micro-wave technology in the development of communications systems which allow almost instantaneous transfer of information on a global basis. These advances point to further extensive development of electronic mail and home shopping. They make probable the universal use in business of desk-top and lap-top computers, telefax machines, communicating word processors, video conferencing etc., and a corresponding reduction in both numbers of office and other staff, and the need for those still employed to make routine daily trips to their office.

In 1992 British Telecom launched an experiment in the Scottish Highlands which involved supplying staff with the necessary communications equipment so that they could operate on a full time basis from home. The experiment was monitored independently to study psychological and other reactions to the new working arrangements. If successful BT suggested that some two million workers throughout Europe could quickly be affected. Meanwhile in addition to direct job losses in telecommunications from other technical change such as electronic switchboarding, a BT spokesman suggested that following a loss of 29,000 jobs in 1992, it was expected that "job shedding should settle down to around 15,000 a year for the next few years". (22)

The implications then for large scale unemployment resulting from technological change in those two areas alone, and quite independent of continuing economic cycles, appears very serious indeed.

With this as background, it is easier to understand why the trend in unemployment has been steadily upwards for more than two decades, and why it might be expected to accelerate.

Certainly there will be new jobs created. There will be the need for "more and more people to build, design, program, install, maintain and operate these robots – jobs which are less boring, dangerous or demoralising than those previously existing". (23) And almost certainly this will be true in other areas affected by technology and as industry and governments make some response to the environmental problem. But it is simply unrealistic to imagine that such new job creation will remotely be sufficient to restore a potential for "full employment" in jobs that pay wages and salaries. Obviously such an outcome poses yet a further threat to the survival of the current financial/economic system; since it relies overwhelmingly on employment related wages and salaries to provide the consumer purchasing power that will allow even the prospect that markets will "clear".

We have seen therefore how the system both causes, and is assailed by, the unsustainability of the exponential growth on which it relies and which is reflected in accelerating international indebtedness and a deteriorating global environment. Now we note how the impending breakdown of the employment mechanism, through which the greatest share of purchasing power is currently delivered to consumers, makes the prospect of system collapse even more certain. But there is yet a further serious threat to the system – disintegrating social cohesion – which we should note before we move to consider how it might be radically reformed in order to resolve these and other problems.

Notes

1. Richardson & Snyder   1984 p. 2/7
2. Maddison A.   1982 p. 56
3. Hixson W.   1991 p. 176
4. Mansfield E.   1969 p. 10
5. Kuznets S.   1966 p. 8
6. Mansfield E.   1969 p. 3
7. Jones B.   1982 p. 36
8. De Màre E.   1986 p. 10
9. Jones B.   1982 p. 139
10. ILO Year Books
11. ILO Year Books
12. MMTA(Machine Tools Stats)   1991 p. 14
13. MMTA(MTE)   1991
14. BIFU Literature   1990/92/93
15. BIFU Literature   1990/92/93
16. BIFU Literature   1990/92/93
17. Scott P.   1984 p. 279
18. Evans C.   1979 p. 148
19.) 15th. Symposium on
20.) Industrial   1985
21.) Robots
22. *The Scotsman*   1992 (July 20th)
23. 15th Symposium on Industrial Robots   1985

CHAPTER

5

SOCIAL BREAKDOWN

As international economies are racked by rising unemployment, unprecedented levels of debt and the effects of a desperately ailing global environment, so the combined impact of these massive problems is experienced as increasing poverty, or in some other way by almost every individual on earth. Social cohesion is under great stress almost everywhere and as the millenium approaches, the optimism of the 1950s and early 60s has given way to a deepening pessimism about our economic and ecological future.

Even in times of full employment, which the developed countries enjoyed for nearly three decades following the end of the second World War, there was poverty and deprivation. But those affected were relatively fewer in number. Their condition could be alleviated by systems of social security, designed to cope with the short term periods of unemployment from full time jobs, which characterised the industrial economies during that period.

The rest of industrial society enjoyed in large measure, continuity of employment for those in the labour force. With it came a sense of security, personal worth and a regular income which allowed them, and their dependents, some claim to a share of the fruits of growing prosperity.

Until the early 1970s, this balance of full employment and social expenditure on unemployment benefit, housing, health, education, and care for the elderly and disabled etc. helped to consolidate a sense of social solidarity. Despite occasional and sometimes serious social unrest, arising especially from local racial tensions or industrial strife, there was still a broad sense of underlying progress and optimism about future prospects. The perception was that crime was not yet a significant everyday concern, at least for the middle classes, and the drug problem was largely a matter of alchohol abuse. That there was an impending global enviromental problem hardly entered the conciousness of the mass of people.

The widespread bitter poverty of the 1930s and its associated ills of hunger, chronic ill health, poor housing, illiteracy, high child mortality and low levels of life expectancy, had finally been left behind. Certainly these might still be the lot of the peoples of the Third World. But to the extent that they were considered important by the people of the industrial North, it was thought that their condition would be most effectively alleviated by trade and other spin offs from a further dash for economic growth by the already industrialised countries.

In the second half of the 1990s however, the world faces an altogether different scenario in which a number of major inter-related problems with global implications are growing rapidly and simultaneously. And at the centre of this network of problems is **the debt-money system and its insatiable need for exponential growth in order to sustain it**.

The traditional view is that economic growth is the key to increased wealth, the restoration of satisfactory levels of employment and an increase in the sum of human happiness. But as we have seen, it is also closely related to cyclical and technological unemployment, a deteriorating global environment and escalating international debt. Together these have in turn given rise to an expansion of poverty, social insecurity and stress, trade in drugs, crime and economic migration etc. Each affects and feeds back upon the other.

Exponential economic growth leads to debt, environmental degradation and unemployment; unemployment and environmental degradation lead to insecurity, poverty and economic migration; economic migration leads to insecurity and ethnic tensions; poverty leads to environmental degradation, escalating debt, a growth in demand for drugs and crime; debt leads to environmental degradation, reduced expenditure on social services, the cultivation and supply of drugs and crime; reducing social expenditure leads to ill health, poverty and insecurity. And so the wheel of misfortune, already spinning at great speed, continues to gather momentum.

This cycle of interlocking problems is now visible to virtually all who would see them. They have generated internationally a widespread, deeply felt apprehension that they may be unmanageable and a related growing pessimism about the kind of future that human beings face.

UNEMPLOYMENT AND POVERTY

We noted in the last chapter that, as the result of a combination of the economic cycle and technological change, unemployment is rising across the industrialised world. There is a slowly growing, albeit still reluctant, acceptance that "full employment" just might never again be possible and that the positive phases of future economic cycles will instead be represented by periods of "jobless recovery". Meanwhile governments' responses almost everywhere are limited to the the concept of retraining the unemployed and to developing "flexibility" in labour markets so as to restore international "competitiveness".

The result of the latter has been the diminishing power of trade unions and an economic environment conducive to the spread of alternative forms of employment and low pay for many of those still in work.

These new work arrangements include increasing part-time, short-term and even "zero hour contracts", of which the last allow for employees to be called to work at a moment's notice when business is good.

A survey by the Low Pay Network based in Manchester, which was reported widely in the UK media in June 1995, confirmed that during a period of economic "recovery" in Britain, such temporary work had risen by 9.9 per cent between 1992 and 1994 while employment rose generally by 0.7 per cent.

These trends are further reinforced as firms throughout the world strive to become ever more competitive. They are driven to substitute capital for labour and/or to shift to locations where labour can be employed more cheaply, while those who retain their jobs on a full time basis are increasingly being expected to work harder and for longer hours.

The new conditions are attended therefore by increasing levels of insecurity and stress. Even those who continue to enjoy relatively secure, well paid jobs and comfortable life styles are becoming concerned about job prospects for their children. They are increasingly made aware that even educational advantage and "contacts"are no longer the guarantee of employment they once were.

Meanwhile the monetarist policies of Western governments which encouraged this labour "flexibility", also underline the need for balanced budgets designed to put a brake on their growing indebtedness. To this end they have embarked upon radical reform of social security systems, including "efficiency" related cut backs in expenditure on unemployment relief, health care, education and housing. This has been supplemented by a determined drive to privatise those "commanding heights" of the economy that had previously been owned and operated(not always successfully) by governments on behalf of their people. The result of these policies however has simply been to further increase poverty, insecurity and unemployment.

As Alf Young, economics editor of *The Herald* newspaper recognised "Growth or no growth, more and more people are living in fear of losing their ticket to economic viability... [and]... People want answers to their deeper fears. And one of the deepest is where work will come from in the future, not just for themselves but for their children". (1) In the summary to their report *For Richer: For Poorer – Changing Distribution of Income in UK 1961 – 1991*, the Institute of Fiscal Studies confirm that "The emergence of mass unemployment has had a major effect on income distribution. Families with children now make up more than half of the poorest decile group compared with only a third three decades ago, with the main reason for this change being the more than eightfold increase in unemployment between the early 1960s and the mid-1980s." (2)

Meanwhile in the third world, unemployment is also one of the most pressing problems facing governments and people.

It is estimated that in countries of the developing South, where great numbers live at subsistence level by working the land or the sea, "unemployment and under-employment runs at some 45% compared to 15% in countries of the North". (3).

International debt ensures economic activity is orientated to exports and, together with rapidly growing populations and poverty, is giving rise to deforestation, destruction of fisheries, desertification, water shortages, and a corresponding further increase in the loss of opportunities for earning a living and related poverty. The critical link between this loss of land and water from overuse and unemployment and poverty, is well made by Paul Harrison when he insists that "All the threats to the land, with the possible exception of salinization, are caused by poverty and overpopulation... land is essential for food and for work... [and]... Loss of land is one of the processes undermining the livelihoods of the rural poor in the Third World. We have seen the others at work in all three continents:the dispossession of smallholders, increasing landlessness, mechanisation, increasing population. Taken together, these trends add up to a rise of terrifying proportions in the numbers of families unable to **find enough work** to feed themselves". (4) (emphasis added)

Similarly where monetarist policies have also been imposed on developing countries by the IMF and World Bank as conditions attached to structural adjustment programs, they too have aggravated the problems of unemployment, poverty and debt. Anna Isla for example notes that as a result of these stabilisation policies, "Latin American countries have become victims of "stagflation", a combination of economic stagnation and inflation. With successive devaluations, in order to make the country's exports more competitive, the purchasing power of wages and salaries is weakened. Per capita income has fallen by 15 per cent, and 44 per cent of the work force is estimated to be unemployed or under-employed. In Peru, per capita monthly income is $41.00... [and]... 70 per cent of the workforce is **unemployed or underemployed** and, according to the UN, 10 million are living on only 10 centavos per day". (5) (emphasise added)

Indeed as the level and duration of unemployment and under-employment continues to rise almost everywhere, so there is an alarming increase in the scale and extent of poverty. In the UK for example, while accepting that there is considerable debate about the definition and scale of poverty, the London based *Family Policy Studies Centre* is clear that the link between unemployment and poverty is a powerful one and there is little doubt that "On all measures and definitions presented here, there was a large rise in poverty during the 1980s in this country". (6)

In dealing with the American experience in *Fighting Poverty* (7), editors Danziger and Weinberg note, quoting Rebecca Blank and Alan Blinder, that "while a permanent increase in the growth rate of per capita income would... probably do wonderful things for the poor, no one has any idea how to achieve it". They go on to say that "The authors find that unemployment, not inflation, is the larger contributor to poverty:a one percentage point increase in unemployment has seven times the effect of a one percentage point decrease in inflation" and they then note that "Had unemployment and inflation not increased over the 1973-1983 decade, Blank and Blinder estimate that the official poverty rate among persons would have fallen from 11.1 to 10.7 per cent instead of rising to 15.2 per cent. Most of that increase was due to unemployment".

Whatever the proximate cause, there is simply no doubt about **the fact of growing poverty**. Hermione Parker (8) for example, quoting from *Hansard*, notes that in the UK in 1983 "an estimated 14 million persons (some 25 per cent of the population) were living in families dependent on family income supplement, housing benefit or supplementary benefit." She continues, quoting from a subsequent issue of *Hansard* that "Since 1985 the situation has got worse. In November 1987, in reply to a Parliamentry Written Question, the Minister estimated that about 4.9 million families with 3.3 million dependents were receiving Supplementary Benefit in 1986, and a further 3.7 million families were receiving standard housing benefit". Her estimate then, on the basis of an unchanged ratio since 1983, is that the total number of persons dependent on

Family Income Supplement, Supplementary Benefit and Housing Benefit in 1986 must have been in the region of 17 million – or about 31 per cent of the population and that some further 5 million persons, or nearly 10 per cent of the population may have been eligible but not claimimg, so that "by 1986 an incredible 40 per cent of the population would have been in receipt of withdrawable benefits, if the take up had been 100 per cent". It is hardly surprising therefore that such poverty, allied to other problems such as crime and drugs which we shall note below, should be accompanied with increasing evidence of family breakdown and associated homelessness and rising levels of single parenthood.

On a global basis it is estimated that poverty entraps more than one billion people or some 20 per cent of the world's population, and that whereas the poor in the North may be able to survive on the basis of "the safety net of social services... [so that] their poverty can be seen as "extreme social deprivation", in the South... the term "absolute poverty" is the only one applicable". (9)

This problem of poverty is now increasingly seen to be such a threat to international stability that the United Nations was persuaded to launch, in March 1995 in Copenhagen, its "Social Summit".

The Secretary General, Boutros Boutros-Ghali in his opening address confirmed that extreme poverty suffered by 1.3 billion people who were without jobs or basic necessities, **was a direct cause of war**. The conference agenda noted that a further 700 million people are under-employed, working long hours for wages that do not cover basic needs.

The Summit was designed therefore to persuade governments that if there was to be the prospect of peace in the world, there must be a serious and successful attempt by them to eradicate world poverty and unemployment. Thousands of non-government organisations, involving aid workers, environmentalists, doctors and many other activists also gathered at another venue in the city to increase the pressure, especially on governments, to ensure that the UN objectives are met.

Yet, while ensuring in this way a greater awareness that a huge international problem exists might increase pressure on governments from their electorates, just as the Rio Summit did in respect of the environmental crisis, media observers were not too impressed with the Social Summit's prospects for success. Trevor Royle (10) considered the Summit a "grandiose and expensive public relations exercise which will do absolutely nothing to stop the suffering and the starving in the world's poorest countries". Other responses encapsulated in press headlines such as "Air of futility drowns out brave words at poverty summit" and "Poverty summit faces uphill fight for soul of UN" suggest that any alleviation even of these problems may be very slow in coming. Meanwhile *Population Concern* is reported as estimating that "by 2030, 70 per cent of the population increase will occur in the very poorest developing countries where average income is less than $2 per day". (11)

Poverty then is a massive and growing problem in the Third World and is also, as we have seen, increasingly serious in the developed countries. It should be clear that the existence of poverty on such a scale will not simply be endured indefinitely by those who suffer from it. Governments around the world are under great and increasing pressure from their own people who are poor or who fear poverty, to do something significant about it. The industrialised countries also face what promises to be an increasingly massive problem of dealing with those in the Third World who are not content to await change at home, but seek to escape their poverty by migration beyond their own frontiers to the rich North.

ECONOMIC MIGRATION

Large numbers traditionally have attempted to escape from poverty, environmental degradation and other related problems by internal migration from rural areas to the cities. As pressure has grown however, national boundaries no longer represent insurmountable obstacles and, despite heightened surveillance, determined migrants now make the journey in increasingly large numbers from poor to rich countries. The accelerating scale and changing nature of the phenomenon represents a further very major threat to international economic and social stability.

Paul Harrison notes that in 1940 for example, "Third World towns and cities housed 185 million people. By 1975, the number had risen to 770 million. In 1960 the UN estimated some 9.2 million people a year were flooding into the Third World cities – some 25,000 every single day. By the early seventies, 12 million people a year – 33,000 per day – were arriving". (12) And Jonathon Porritt, in *Save the Earth* estimates that as a result of migration to Third World cities, and growth within those cities, **"59 per cent of the world's population in the year 2025 will live in urban areas"** (13) (emphasis added), with all the consequencies that seem to accompany such rapid urbanisation – massive overcrowding in slum housing, poor sanitation, malnutrition, disease, gross pollution, crime, drug abuse and growing tensions between established city dwellers and incomers.

Great numbers of migrant workers are also already on the move north and west from the Third World, pressing to gain access to the countries of the rich First World. Since the the end of the second world war, estimates of the scale of legal and illegal migration have been constantly increasing until today they have become a major source of alarm for the developed countries. Paul Harrison refers to "A steady stream of workers... [flowing]... north and west from the Third World into the rich First World... [and that]... in the sixties, the UN-affiliated ILO estimated 5.1 million migrants from poor countries joined this long treck for work. In 1980 some estimates put their numbers as high as 20 million". (14)

By 1992, Susan George et al. were also observing in *The DEBT BOOMERANG* that the UN Environment Program (UNEP) expects that there may be a billion environmental refugees early in the next century. Meanwhile they note that millions are faced with "dehumanising poverty, shooting wars, or ecological collapse... [and]... find all their previous means of livelihood vanishing". They go on to ask "What option have they – besides death – but to move?" (15) It is of course not just economic migration from the countries of the poor South that is causing concern.

The Economist (16) for example, suggests that while in Europe the greatest problem is likely to come from across the Mediterannean where... "Earnest

Spanish civil servants already talk of Europe's "southern flank"... [and where]... military overtones, the sense of siege, are unmistakeable... it should also be recognised that... The first rush from Eastern Europe and the Soviet Union has already begun, with roughly 2 million people leaving there last year... [and further that]... As unemployment sweeps through eastern Europe and the Soviet Union disintegrates, the numbers may continue in the low millions in each year of the 1990s".

It is of course not just the poor who are on the move. Those in the developed countries who can afford to move are also flitting in increasing numbers. Many are fleeing, from the inner cities and areas in which the communities are now largely composed of immigrants, to escape from what they see as the worst effects of large scale immigration, social breakdown and general economic failure. Their movement too often increases tension.

So as we approach the millenium, there is very great and growing concern in the industrialised countries, especially within the European Community and North America, about the threat to economic stability and social cohesion that will result if this perceived potential for further mass in-migration, especially from the poor countries of North Africa, Eastern Europe, Asia, South America and the Carribean is realised. While France has now begun to respond more positively to this problem by offering "people centered" financial and technical assistance to some of its old colonies in North Africa, the broad consensus amongst mainstream politicians elsewhere remains simply that the "correct" response involves little more than liberal immigration laws, acceptance without debate by host communities of the idea of a multi-ethnic, multi-cultural identity, and a new legal concept of "civic nationalism". Meanwhile on a global basis there is a growing fear that nation states and national identities are to be subsumed in the emerging regional economic blocs and replaced with a new more easily manipulated "identity" based on economic interest. There is a growing anxiety too about the prospect, as power is increasingly centralised, that policy direction will be exercised by bankers operating via independent central banks; that policy implementation will be the province of powerful and permanent bureaucracies and that real democracy will simply become impractical.

And to make matters worse, at the same time as unemployment, poverty, debt, and environmental damage are propelling huge numbers of people to seek respite in cities and in the developed world where they simply cannot be accommodated, there are also large numbers who seek a solution to their economic problems not by migration but by involvement in some way in the cultivation, trade, or consumption of drugs.

TRADE IN DRUGS

Although the problem of drugs abuse is an old one, the huge rise in international debt and poverty has contributed greatly to a massive increase in trade in illegal drugs and associated crime.

In America, sources quoted by Peter Andreas and Humberto Campodonico (17) suggest that in 1989 "a record number of Americans – 64 per cent – cited drugs as the number one problem of the United States". They report that crimes of violence, including an increased number of murders and a wave of drug related incidents, had risen by 10 per cent between 1984 and 1990 as part of a six year acceleration in the total crime rate, producing a trend which experts attributed largely to "more drug-related violence."

On a global basis, it is suggested in *Winning the War on Drugs*, that the international trade in illegal drugs "ranks with oil and armaments as one of the world's most valuable and profitable traded commodities" and, quoting Coleman, was in 1989 already worth "some $500 billion per year... [with]... the relatively small group of criminals who now control illegal drugs... having a **bigger turnover than the income of 150 of the world's 170 nations**". (18) (emphasis added)

In Europe there are almost daily reports of huge hauls of illegal drugs being intercepted by drug enforcement organisations and of increasing numbers of deaths from drug related crime and overdosing. While it is the poor who are most adversely affected by the trade in dangerous and "recreational" drugs it is by no means confined to them. There are many, in work and enjoying above average incomes, who resort to illegal drugs as well as alcohol in an attempt to mitigate the increasing levels of stress to which they feel subject.

In fact the United Nations confirm that while drug abuse and illicit trafficking, which have been increasing throughout the world at an alarming rate over the last 25 years, affects primarily the young it also crosses "all social, economic, political and national bounderies". (19)

There is a fairly widely held view that a major contributory factor to the international drug problem is prohibition. While that may well be so, it can surely not be denied that the real roots of the modern drugs crisis are to be found in the poverty, despair and stress endured by such large and increasing numbers of people, as escalating unemployment and international debt has afflicted both the industrialised and developing countries. After all, according to a confirmed supporter of drug legalisation, during a continuous period of 70 years of prohibition "drugs use increased only slowly until the 1960s and then rapidly". (20)

It can hardly be a simple coincidence that the 1960s saw both the end of the post-war economic boom, as the destruction of World War II was repaired, and the beginning of the rapid descent into economic malaise, unemployment and poverty that has followed the oil crises and the crushing growth in the recurring burden of international debt.

There is for example, little doubt in the minds of the previously quoted P. Andreas and H. Campodonico about the importance of the link between debt and the drugs trade. They insist, that although the debt crisis might not have been the direct cause of the drugs crisis, they are certain their research shows that recourse to drug production and trade has undoubtedly been fuelled by debt and they stress that "any alternative drug control strategy abroad must, necessarily, include major debt relief". (21)

Similarly, the UN make the link between the drug trade and poverty, albeit in typically restrained language, in their resolution 47/99 of 1992 when they comment "that there are obvious links, under certain circumstances, between poverty and the increase in the illicit production and trafficking of narcotic and psychotropic substances and that policies of alternative economic development

can make a contribution in addressing this problem". (22)

There is less of a conditionality when they go on to note the link between drugs and crime and their effect on society.

In this context they are certain that "Drugs trafficking has become very sophisticated and complex, involving organised crime in a variety of illegal activities, including conspiracy, bribery, intimidation and corruption of public servants, tax evasion, banking law violations, racketeering, illegal money transfers, import/export violations, smuggling of weapons, crimes of violence and terrorism. Drug-related problems thus directly affect social stability and public safety and are associated with social disintegration." (23)

CRIME

Crime is also a very complex social phenomenon. It has a number of causes in addition to the trade in illicit drugs. It too is perpetrated by and affects the affluent as well as the poor. There is considerable debate about what triggers rising levels of crime. Most people, applying "common sense" to the problem, would be quite certain that there was at least some direct and positive relationship between levels of unemployment and levels of crime in society. But research results from the 1920s onwards have often been contradictory or inconclusive.

In their book *Unemployment Crime and Offenders*, Crow et al. note that, as early as 1922 "a relationship was reported between criminal conviction rates and the index of business activity in the United States... [and that]... A study of the business cycle for the first half of the twentieth century showed a substantial correlation between low levels of business activity and high levels of property crime"; that in 1940 a "study by Mannheim... found that the movement of crime corresponds fairly accurately to fluctuations of unemployment"; that a study by Fleisher in 1963 concludes that "An examination of delinquency rates and other variables by age and through time suggests that the effect of unemployment on juvenile delinquency is positive and significant"; that "subsequent evidence on unemployment, age and crime has tended to support these conclusions".

On the other hand they also note that "We have recorded over twenty references which relate specifically to this issue and a Home Office researcher reviewing the literature examined thirty studies. They came to widely differing conclusions. A few writers believe the link is negligible. At the other extreme are a small number of studies which conclude that unemployment is a major crime-producing agent". (24)

Despite the conflicting conclusions of these and many other studies it seems to be generally accepted that common sense is a more reliable guide and that unemployment does in fact lead to increased levels of crime. It is however by no means the only or necessarily the proximate or most significant factor in all cases.

Drug abuse for example has increasingly been linked with crime (trafficking, theft, intimidation and violence, money laundering, bribery etc.). Poverty reflecting unemployment, falling levels of welfare payments, other social provision and related homelessness and family breakdown also often lead to crime. At the same time the development of technology and sophisticated vehicles such as derivatives, for financial speculation on a grand scale, have led to a rapid rise in "white collar" crime. The collapse of Barings bank in 1995 was just one of the more spectacular of recent examples.

Whatever the causes, crime is growing rapidly throughout the world. In the United Kingdom the rise in notifiable offences recorded by the police rose from 3.435 million in 1981 to 6. 133 million in 1993. (25) The United Nations estimated in 1990 that "For every 100 recorded crimes in 1975, there would be 160 in the year 2000; for every 100 police officers there would be 170; and for every 100 adults in prison, there would be over 200... [and]... rising levels of recorded crime and of State responses to it can be expected to have a significant and deleterious effect on many national economies by the year 2000. The harm done to individual victims may not easily be quantified in economic terms, but organised crime – and with it a threat to legitimate business practices – seems likely to grow". (26)

ENVIRONMENT

As if continuously rising levels of unemployment, poverty, drugs and crime were not already a sufficiently formidable list of afflictions borne by peoples in almost every country in the world, another even more fundamentally serious problem has to be added – the daily more immediate and obvious signs that our planet Earth is being pushed beyond the point at which the human life support systems can continue to operate.

The scale of the problem has been reviewed in a previous chapter. But for the most part it is not until the last few years and the massive development in global communications, that increasing numbers of people have really begun to understand and accept that the damage being done to the earth is not only seriously affecting them now, but that there is a real prospect that it may, for humans, soon prove terminal.

Television brings the fact of recurring famine and drought into our living rooms with increasing frequency. Almost everyone now knows about the hole in the Ozone Layer. If they are not sure about the technical details they are well aware that it is a problem of great significance to life on earth.

Epidemics of respiratory ailments, dying forests, diminishing fresh water fish stocks and the every day experience of city and suburban life, bring home almost daily to each of us that forecasts of the deadly effects of pollution from acid-laden rain, black snow and the oxides from car exhausts, have been more than fully justified.

Plagues of jellyfish, great tides of toxic algae, hundreds upon hundreds of dead dolphins washing up on Mediterranean beaches, the threatened extinction of much marine life, from the tiny anchovy to some of the great whales, and the dramatically declining levels of fish stocks in virtually every marine fishery around the world make the news on an almost daily basis.

From an article in *Worldwatch* magazine "Where have all the Rivers Gone?" the *Scotsman* newspaper notes that "In Arizona the Salt and Gila rivers used to join west of Phoenix. Today they dry up east of the city as thirsty farms divert their waters. In China, the Heaven River near Beijing dried up twenty years ago.

A portion of the Yellow River, which earned a reputation as "China's Sorrow" because of its frequent flooding, is now dry near its mouth in Shandong Province during the dry season. In the Middle East, the Jordan River is so overused that the lower stretches are no more than a trickle." (27)

Specialist programs on television such as *Icon Earth* transmitted on BBC in March 1995 and distributed to other international TV networks confirm for millions of viewers that the experience of the astronauts in Apollo 13, as their life support systems began to fail before it exploded some 200,000 miles out in space, is not dissimilar to our own on earth – "The farmer, the fisherman, the businessman and the housewife, the car worker, the unemployed and you and I face a similar crisis, and one way or another we have to find some answers". (28)

This contention that there is rapidly growing awareness and concern about the devastating potential of our abuse of the global environment is well supported by the rise in involvement and membership of voluntary environmental organisations over the last 25 years or so. In the United Kingdom alone, between 1971 to 1993 membership of Greenpeace grew from nil to 410,000; Friends of the Earth from 1,000 to 120,000; Royal Society for Nature Conservation from 64,000 to 248,000 and the World Wide Fund for Nature from 12,000 to 207,000. (29)

And, whatever the technical merits, the massive response by citizens throughout Europe to the proposal by Shell UK. and the British government to sink the obsolete Brent Spar oil platform in the Atlantic, just 150 miles from the Scottish coast, was dramatic confirmation that there is deep, widespread and growing concern about the global environmental issue.

In the face of this network of interlocking social problems, which seem destined only to get worse as the years go by, it cannot be surprising that greed, stress, anxiety, pessimism and fear of violence are spreading like a miasma through modern society. In Britain, once proud of its unique "cradle to the grave" welfare provision, the gap between rich and poor continues to widen inexorably, and senior executives rake in huge salary increases and share option gains while staff are dismissed in pursuit of "efficiency". Meanwhile poverty and hopelessness are like tinder in our inner cities. Despite three decades of economic growth, the UK. media can report in June 1995 that a survey commissioned by the children's charity Barnardos, confirms that two out of three adults believe that children today are inheriting a world worse than that of their parents. On every issue relating to the prospects for their children – level of violence, opportunities for rewarding careers, potential for a stable family life, security at school etc. – parents believe that their children will be worse off than they have been.

No one is immune from the implications of this deteriorating sense of social solidarity.

It is important therefore to emphasise again that these problems do not arise solely from the implementation of specific political ideologies and associated orthodox economic prescriptions. **After all, as we have already noted, each of the competing orthodox economic/political policies have been pursued** *simultaneously* **over some 15 years in Britain by a Conservative government; for extensive periods in Australia, France and Spain by**

Socialist governments; in Canada by Conservative and Liberal governments and in America by Republican and Democrat governments – and everywhere the results have been almost identical.

It should be clear therefore that no change of government can provide the basis for a constructive resolution of our plight, unless it is accompanied by the radical restructuring of the money system.

Notes

1. Young A. (*Herald*)   1992 (Nov 2nd)
2. Goodman A. & Webb S.   1994 p. 66
3. Myers N. (Ed.)   1994 p. 179
4. Harrison P.   1993 p. 134/5
5. Isla A.   1993
6. Roll J.   1992 p. 43
7. Danziger S. H. & Weinberg D. H.   1986 p. 10
8. Parker H.   1989 p. 55/57
9. Myers N. (Ed.)   1994 p. 216
10. Royle T. (*Scotland on Sunday*)   1995 (Mar 12th)
11. *Scotland on Sunday*   1995 (Mar 5th)
12. Harrison P.   1993 p. 145
13. Porritt J. et al.   1991 p. 125
14. Harrison P.   1993 p. 141
15. George S.   1992 p. 112
16. *The Economist*   1991 p. 12
17. George S.   1992 p. 34
18. Stevenson R.   1994 p. 17/74
19. United Nations   1990 p. 322
20. Stevenson R.   1994 p. 17
21. George S.   1992 p. 62
22. United Nations   1992 p. 916
23. United Nations   1990 p. 324
24. Crow I. et al.   1989 p. 2/4
25. *Social Trends 25*   1995 p. 154
26. United Nations   1990 p. 320
27. *The Scotsman*   1995 (July 18th)
28. Icon Earth   1995
29. *Social Trends 25*   1995 Table 11.4

CHAPTER

6

SUMMARY

Orthodox economics comprises a number of competing "schools" whose basic differences have been narrowed down, especially over the last twenty or thirty years, so that the major remaining difference of principle is now whether, and to what extent, markets clear automatically.

The world however continues to be beset by the same economic problems that have afflicted it, with only brief periods of respite, since at least the beginning of the industrial revolution. Today those problems – unemployment, poverty, international debt, destruction of the global environment etc. – when taken together are of significantly greater magnitude than ever before.

Governments everywhere, of every political complexion and irrespective of which school of orthodox economics they elect to follow, can find no lasting or satisfactory solution to any of them. "Economic growth", repeated like some sacred mantra, has become their only hope despite the mounting evidence that continuous economic growth is actually making matters worse rather than better.

Yet economic orthodoxy either fudges or steadfastly refuses to consider at all, **the root cause** of these problems – **the creation and destruction of credit by private banks on the basis of the fractional reserve/debt-money system which the whole world uses and which is simply unsustainable**.

This exclusion of the debt-money system from any detailed consideration by the economics profession and by politicians is a critical omission.

Its importance should be obvious when we note that the debt- money system is the extraordinary arrangement whereby private commercial banks are allowed the authority to create credit (debt/money) "out of nothing" on the basis of their "fractional reserves". That is each pound of legal tender money created by government, when deposited in a clearing bank, allows that bank to create up to some nine additional pounds in loans to individuals, businesses and governments! These newly created funds exist only as deposits/loans in the records of the banks and they are simply cancelled from those records, and **removed from the economy**, when the loans and related interest are repaid. They are not real money in the sense that notes and coins are, and they are not legal tender.

Yet borrowers must repay this "money", which banks create out of nothing and lend into circulation, **plus interest for which at the time no money has been created**.

There is therefore a continuous deficiency of money (consumer purchasing power), and a corresponding periodic surplus of goods in the economy.

Distribution of this surplus and the production of subsequent goods, can be temporarily arranged by persuading consumers to borrow against future income. It can also be arranged by ensuring a further round of borrowing by governments and entrepreneurs to finance a further round of economic activity. But with each successive round of consumer borrowing or economic activity, outstanding interest from the last round must be met. The result therefore is an ever bigger surplus of goods at the end of each successive round. There is a corresponding escalation in the total of outstanding debt and interest on debt.

Eventually the debt cannot be fully met; there is a widespread threat of debt repudiation and the system breaks down. These periodic break downs or recessions, which involve mass unemployment and business bankruptcies, usually allow the accrued surpluses gradually to be run down. The process is commonly accompanied by an atmosphere of industrial and social strife.

Whatever the route however, the system eventually returns as it must, to the pursuit of renewed exponential economic growth. Through each period of expansion and contraction **surpluses, prices, unemployment and the total of world debt and debt interest spiral ever upward**. The impact of the recurring recessions, **superimposed on these series of rising trends**, gradually also becomes more severe and they are transformed at longer intervals into depressions, which are so intractable that the only "solution" in the past has been the destruction of unmanageable surpluses by recourse to the "capture of export markets" and eventually military war.

And yet despite these inevitable and destructive effects, for so long as the current debt-money system is allowed to continue, then for so long will exponential economic growth have to be pursued. It is the only way that bankers can conceive to ensure that increasing levels of debt plus interest can be repaid to them and that their system might survive.

It matters not to them that governments must cut back their borrowing and public expenditure; that the depression of business activity leads to bankruptcies and cyclical unemployment; that businesses are driven to reduce costs by replacing labour with technology or by relocation to where cheaper labour is available so that further impetus is given to unemployment; that poverty, economic migration, drug abuse and crime increase dramatically and that the threat of destruction of the global environment and the human life support systems is dramatically accelerated.

Why politicians and economists operating within the prevailing orthodoxy fail to consider these aspects of this critical mechanism in the economic system is something of a mystery.

It may be as Count Tolstoy suggested, "that most men including those at ease with highly complex problems, can rarely accept even the simplest and most obvious truth if to do so should require them to admit the falsity of conclusions that they have delighted in explaining to colleagues, which they have proudly taught to others, and which they have woven, thread by thread, into the fabric of their lives." (1)

It may be as Professor Ormerod suggests, that economics so dominates current political debate to the extent "that it is scarcely possible to have a serious political career in many Western countries without being able to repeat more or less accurately its current fashionable orthodoxies... (and that) The obstacles facing academic economists are formidable, for tenure and professional advancement still depend to a large extent on a willingness to comply with and work within the tenets of orthodox theory". (2)

What is certain, is that over the last few centuries the banking fraternity have fought an unremitting and so far successful battle to establish and maintain their effective monopoly in the creation of the world's money supply. Their success has provided them with a base of immense power and influence from which it will be difficult to dislodge them.

No matter how difficult however, the debt-money system must be subjected to detailed analysis and radical reform, if there is to be the slightest hope that the problems dealt with in the first part of this book can be satisfactorily resolved.

Part 2 will show that awareness of the need for such reform has a long history and is in fact again gathering support around the world. It will review the progress of international bankers to the position of dominant power which they now enjoy, and it will deal with some of the most important analyses and proposals for change that have been made by critics of fractional reserve banking.

Finally it will present a Plan for Action and a call for co-operation so that the necessary reforms are implemented.

Notes
1. Gleick J.   1987 p. 38
2. Ormerod P.   1994 p. x/4

PART
2

THE ROUTE TO CHANGE

CHAPTER
7

THE HISTORIC STRUGGLE FOR CHANGE

Robertson, in *Human Ecology*, suggests that when a mechanism is examined, the questions automatically arise – "who created this mechanism, and for what purpose". (1) He goes on to suggest that nearly all monetary reformers consider that the current debt-money system has been deliberately created to reflect some conscious design of an individual or group of men. He is inclined to reject this proposition however and, in support of his rejection, quotes Sir Arthur Salter (author of *Recovery*) as follows:

> To imagine that at the centre of the intricate web of man's economic activities stand a few constructive and controlling intelligences is to entertain a romantic illusion. There are no such Olympians. The intricate system of finance has been built and is operated by thousands of men of keen but limited vision, each working within the limit of his own special sphere... Those who have made and worked the system have normally not understood it as a whole... The economic and financial structure under which we have grown up is... (more)... like one of the marvellously intricate structures built up by the instincts of beavers or ants than the deliberately designed and rational works of man. (2)

On the other hand De Màre (3) offers, among many, the following quotes from *The Bankers' Magazine* and from the *Financial Times* to suggest the opposite. These might at least give us pause before we decide whether or not to concur with Thomas Robertson in this matter:

> Whoever may be the indiscreet Minister who revives the money-trust bogey at a moment when the Government has most need to be polite to the banks, should be put through an elementary course of instruction, in fact as well as in manners. Does he, do his colleages, realise that half a dozen men at the top of the big five banks could upset the whole fabric of Government finance by refraining from renewing Treasury Bills?
>
> (*Financial Times*, September 26th 1921)

Capital must protect itself in every possible manner by combination and legislation. Debts must be collected, bonds and mortgages must be foreclosed as rapidly as possible. When, through a process of law, common people lose their homes, they will become more docile and more easily governed through the influence of the strong arm of government, applied by a central power of wealth under control of leading financiers. This truth is well known among our principal men now engaged in forming an imperialism of capital to govern the world.

(*The Bankers' Magazine of USA*, August 26th 1924)

Whether the system is in fact the result of a conscious continuing conspiracy or indeed has "just growed" like Topsy hardly matters. The destructive effects of money-lending at interest have been evident and opposed for thousands of years. In the Old Testament for example we note... " We have borrowed money for the kings tribute and that upon our lands and vineyards... and lo, we bring into bondage our sons and our daughters to be servants... neither is it in our power to redeem them; for other men have our lands and vineyards". (*Nehemiah V 1-12*) Plus ca change!

Robertson (4) shows clearly that there has been unremitting criticism of usury for many centuries and suggests that such opposition to the debt-money system makes up virtually the entire history of the European continent. Indeed he insists that any objective review of the facts will confirm that nearly all war and civil strife, "from the internecine struggles of the Greek city states, through the rise and fall of Athens and of Rome, on to the wars of Napoleon, were simply misdirected efforts to escape the bondage of the usurers". And he asks too, "what was the 1914 World War, the Russian revolution, the rise of the totalitarian state, but the same opposition to the pressure of centralised debt?" Certainly the following review of the last couple of hundred years or so would tend to support this proposition.

RECURRING CRISES; THE GREAT DEPRESSION AND RENEWED OPPOSITION TO THE DEBT-MONEY SYSTEM

In the period following the Napoleonic Wars, European economies were frequently in crisis. In the crisis of 1816/17 some "90 issuing banks went bankrupt between 1816 and 1817" and in that of 1825/26 "70 private issuing banks had to suspend payments when the holders of bank notes tried to convert their notes into gold". (5)

Further economic crises followed in 1847 and 1857, while in 1866, had the British government not temporarily suspended the Bank of England's cover regulations (the ratio of gold cover to notes), the Bank would have "had to deny the British economy credit when it was most needed". (6)

The inescapable need of the financial system for exponential growth however ensured that economic expansion continued to accelerate despite these periodic crises. So too did the related total of debt and interest payable on debt continue to escalate and the recurring crises became progressively more serious until the world's financial-economic system was rocked again to its foundations by the

1929 Wall Street Crash and its aftermath.

On October 24th/25th 1929 there was panic selling and a collapse of share prices on the New York Stock Exchange. And for virtually the next decade the world was to be plagued by the effects of the "Great Depression".

Initial intervention by American bankers to control the situation failed and political and financial interests were widely accused of having organised a "give-and-take among themselves without the public being able to do anything to control them" (7). During 1931 alone more than 2000 American banks collapsed and growing distrust and bitterness were directed at the banking community. In 1932 a sub committee of the Banking and Currency Committee of the Senate examined the New York Stock Exchange and the security transactions of New York banks. It found major abuses by major banks, including the sale by the National City Bank of New York to its own customers of securities which the bank itself considered to be unsound!

In Germany as the impact of the Wall Street crash took effect the banks, despite the rules relating to banking prudence, attempted to protect their investments in troubled major industrial companies by offering them further credits.

At the same time the German banks owned large quantities of industrial and commercial shares from their involvement in the creation of trusts during the 1920s. When Chancellor Bruning dissolved Parliament in September 1930, and the resulting election gave the National Socialists nearly 20 per cent of the vote, there began a frantic withdrawal of funds by overseas creditors. The value of stocks and shares nosedived and as a result German banks found themselves in serious difficulty. On May 11th 1931 it became clear that the biggest commercial bank in Austria – Osterreichische Creditanstalt – had suffered huge losses and a major German banking crisis was precipitated.

Although quite badly affected by the German banking crisis, the British and French banking interests apparently weathered the international storm somewhat more comfortably.

That is more than can be said for the business sector and for the great bulk of the populations in these countries and around the world. Commercial bankruptcy, mass unemployment, poverty and hunger, drug abuse, homelessness and family breakdown were the lot of countless millions who just a few years earlier had shared for a short while, especially in America, the optimism of the "Roaring Twenties". Despair, anger and a sense of bitter hopelessness were almost universal.

It is quite remarkable that this kind of financial/economic experience and associated criticism, complaint and attacks upon the system over centuries, should have resulted in an almost complete lack of success in achieving significant reform.

Nevertheless it is very important to recognise that there have indeed been times, usually of economic or political crisis, when the system has come under such keen analysis and powerful attack that it has been shaken to its foundations, often almost to the point of ensuring its total collapse.

In America the monopoly of money creation by bankers was broken for extended periods, as money was created and put into circulation interest free by the governments of individual States and by the Federal Government.

In the Channel Islands and Europe there have been periods during which the successful creation of money by local governments represented such a serious threat to the system and its beneficiaries that they had to be proscribed.

Especially during the inter war years, including the years of the "Great Depression", the debt-money system was the subject of sustained and very powerful attack from a number of quarters around the world. In Canada the first nominally Social Credit government was elected in 1935 with an overwhelming mandate to effect monetary and economic reform. Later following its nationalisation in 1938, the Bank of Canada exercised its constitutional powers to create a very significant proportion of the nation's money supply to "finance federal projects on an near-interest-free basis". (8)

A short review of some of the more interesting and effective of these attempts at reform of the system, will be useful background to discussion of current opposition and the detailed proposals for change which are the subject of the following chapters.

THE GUERNSEY EXPERIMENT

In the immediate aftermath of the Napoleonic Wars the economy of the Island of Guernsey was in desperate decline. The roads were no better than muddy cart tracks, there was little trade and unemployment was a great problem. The sea was washing through dilapidated dykes and sweeping away much of the land. The State's Debt was £19,137 on which annual interest was £2,390. Annual revenue was only £3,000.

So, while great sums of money were needed to repair the sea walls and to kick start the economy, nett resources from current revenue was only £600 per annum.

The dyke repair project alone was estimated to cost £10,000. But in addition, a new covered Public Market was required; extensive road works and a variety of other works were also necessary. Further taxation was simply not possible and clearly neither was borrowing a practical proposition. An appeal to London for funds was refused.

In 1816 the island's Governor appointed a Committee to consider the crisis and it recommended that the expense of acquiring property, building a covered market, some road works etc., should be met by the issue of States Notes of £1 sterling, to a total value of £6,000.

It was suggested in the Committee's report that this was an eminently reasonable proposal "when one considers that the banks already have their notes in circulation for more than £50,000, whereas it is now proposed to restrict the States' issue to a mere £6,000". (9)

In fact £4,000 States Notes were issued later that year for coast preservation works, and were subject to redemption in three stages, April 1817, October 1817, and April 1818 and not for re-issue. In 1820 authority was given for a further issue of £4,500, redeemable in 10 years, to finance the new market. Further issues followed in 1821, 1824, 1826 (when the States of Guernsey £5 Note appeared) and by 1837 the grand total was some £55,000.

The result was that "In the Billet d'Etat it was a frequent subject for congratulations; and it was stated over and over again by eminent men of those times that without the issue of States' Notes, important public works, such as roads and buildings could not have been carried out. Yet by means of the States' issue, not only were these works accomplished, but the Island was not a penny the poorer in interest charges. Indeed, the improvements had stimulated the flow of visitors to the island, and with increased trade the island enjoyed its new found prosperity". (10)

For ten years there was no opposition, but in 1826 as the total of States' Notes in circulation reached £20,000 complaint was made to the Privy Council and an explanation was demanded of the Guernsey authorities. An explanation was duly given and accepted.

However matters changed with the establishment of two private banks on the island, the first in 1827 and the second in 1830, who flooded the island with their own private note issues. The States set up a committee to discuss the matter with the banks but the extraordinary outcome was that the States withdrew £15,000 of their notes from circulation and agreed to limit their issue of States Notes to £40,000 in future!

During the First World War the State's Notes issue was again increased. In 1958 it was reported to have reached a total in circulation of £542,765, (11) although in real terms this represents very little change with the passage of 100 years.

EXPERIMENT IN CONTINENTAL EUROPE

In the depression years of the early 1930s, the towns of Wörgl and Kirchbichel in the Austrian Tyrol, and Swanenkirchen in Bavaria also issued their own money. In Wörgl for example there stood, and probably still stands, a bridge on which there is a plaque commemorating the fact that it was built by debt-free, locally created money.

When the local government recognised that it was virtually bankrupt, a decision was made to issue the town's own money in the form of numbered "labour certificates". The total value of these certificates, issued in various small denominations, was some 30,000 schillings.

These notes, along lines suggested by Sylvio Gesell, depreciated monthly by one per cent of their face value to encourage their rapid circulation. At the end of the month holders of the notes had to fix to the back of the note a stamp bought from the local authority to restore to the note its original face value. The notes were put into circulation by paying them to local authority workers as a significant percentage of their wages, and because they were acceptable by the town in payment of taxes and other dues they were acceptable to virtually all of the businesses in the town. Because of this and their tendency to monthly depreciation, the notes circulated with great speed. Businesses prospered, local unemployment was greatly relieved and, just as in Guernsey, significant new facilities and local infrastructure were provided. News of the "miracle" spread widely and the American economist, Professor Irving Fisher sent a commission of enquiry to Wörgl. Once again however there was opposition from bankers, this time from the Austrian State Bank, and in 1933 the experiment was ended.

REVOLT IN AMERICA

[This short review of the historical reaction to the debt money system in America, is based almost wholly on relevant sections of William F. Hixson's cogent and rigorously argued book *Triumph of the Bankers, Money and Banking in the Eighteenth and Nineteenth Centuries*, published in the USA by Greenwood Publishing Group.]

Within the space of a few years at the end of the 1690s, the Massachusetts Bay Colony had made a first issue of its "colonial notes" and across the Atlantic the Bank of England issued its first commercial "bank notes". These represented therefore the almost simultaneous issue of paper money by government fiat on the one hand and by a private commercial enterprise on the other.

The Massachusetts notes circulated very successfully for some 20 years to supplement gold and silver specie which was scarce. Their success stimulated the introduction of government-issued paper money by other colonies including South Carolina, New Jersey and New York.

In most of these colonies, "when notes were issued except for military expeditions... the notes resulted from loans on land and brought annual interest to the government"(p. 55) and ensured lower taxes than would otherwise have been necessary. In this way, just as in the Guernsey experiment a hundred years later, roads, buildings and other infrastructure projects were constructed without any need for taxation.

It is interesting to note that in 1733 Maryland also put £48,000 of their notes into circulation by "giving away a certain sum to each inhabitant over 15 years of age". (p. 56, quoting Lestor 1939) This exercise anticipated the National Dividend proposals of Major C. H. Douglas in the 1920s which we shall discuss later.

However in due course the British Government, in 1751 and 1763, acting it is suggested on the prompting of money-lenders rather than entrepreneurs or the wider community, moved to forbid further issues of legal tender paper money by the colonists.

This action by the British government simply exacerbated the already significant list of grievances which the colonists held against Britain. Benjamin Franklin continued to defend the government-issue of legal tender paper money by the colonists, but his arguments were rejected by the British Parliament. The result was that by 1773 the total number of new issues of colonial notes had been reduced by half compared to 1764. Subsequently Westminster relented and agreed that the colonies' notes issues could be accepted as legal tender for public payments such as colonial taxes, fines etc – but were **not acceptable** for the settlement of private debts. This remained the position until the outbreak of the War for Independence.

Until 1775, and despite a severe shortage of gold and silver, the colonists had managed to increase their total money supply (specie plus paper) roughly in proportion to output. **Any danger of inflation was therefore avoided.**

However with the advent of war with Britain it became more difficult than ever for them to increase their supply of specie, just as the the need for money to pay for the war skyrocketed. The individual states then, using their previous successful experience of money creation, issued again their own paper money through the Continental Congress.

This time it was "not in proportion to the relatively slow-growing needs of trade but in response to the fast-growing needs of war". (p. 73)

The results were first that the war was largely paid for by the colonists simply by issuing the necessary amounts of paper money. Secondly, **because it was issued in excess of the output of goods and services,** it caused "runaway price inflation".

Hixson comments however that "It is the second of these results that historians ideologically opposed to the issue of paper money by governments have chosen to emphasise and implant indelibly in the minds of their readers"(p. 74). He insists instead that it is much more important to note that the American colonists were able to win the war and assure their independence **only by resorting to government-issued paper money.**

Indeed he insists that rather than any tax on tea, to a significant extent, the war was fought over the right of the colonists to create their own money supply. After all "The right of a people to create their own money through their government was an issue that played a principal role in the real growth of the Colonial economies before 1775.". (p. 81)

Yet following the successful conclusion of the war, the Constitution of the newly independent United States neither authorised nor specifically denied the right of the federal government to issue paper money.

The result was continued and heated debate about the merits of government-issued paper money against those of specie (gold and silver coin) supplemented by private bank-created money, so that from a position where the War for Independence had been won without the existence of private banks, there now began "an unbridled proliferation of private banking... in the decade of the 1790s". (p. 92)

Hixson notes that by 1860, as the Civil War approached, in the States that were to stay loyal to the Union, specie amounted to some 31 per cent of their total money supply. The balancing 69 per cent was in the form of private bank created money – i.e. bank notes and bank deposits or "check-book money". It was to alter dramatically over the next few years following Abraham Lincoln's inauguration as President in March 1861. The Civil war to maintain the Union began in April of that year and a huge increase in the armed forces and related armaments, equipment and supplies led to a corresponding escalation in federal expenditures. The annual cost of the war to the Union grew from $35 million in 1861 to $1,227 million in 1865 and by its end totalled $3,674 millions.

Faced with these enormous sums needed to finance the war and with the prospect of considerable difficulties in borrowing on this scale, "Congress then turned, as had the Continental Congress nearly a century before, to a government emission of paper money". (p. 131)

Government created money – Greenbacks – was used to pay for some 35. 3 per cent of the first three year total cost of $1,164 millions but only 0.7per cent of the second three year total of $2,510 millions.

This decline in the use of Government-issued money to meet the war costs reflects the fact that opposition to government-created money had never been silenced and that "by 1866 the government had ceased creating money; and there was less government-created money in circulation than in 1865". (p. 141)

A key factor in this change was the passage of the National Banking Act in February 1863 whose purpose was publicly declared to be "to provide a National currency, secured by a pledge of United States Stocks, and to provide for circulation and redemption thereof". (p. 142)

But Hixson suggests that the real purpose was more complicated. The issue and circulation of non interest-bearing United States notes in fact already provided a national currency and there was no obvious need for another. Instead the National Banking Act provided for an interest-bearing national currency to be issued by private banks and put into circulation by lending them to borrowers from the bank.

The principal intention of the sponsors of this Banking Act it seems was to ensure as soon as possible the complete withdrawal of Greenbacks, on which no interest was payable, and its replacement by bank issued interest-bearing currency as the only national currency.

Hixson brings his analysis up to the creation of the Federal Reserve System in 1913 when it "in a sense, became the money-creator of last resort... [while]... Banks, of course, remained the money-creator of first resort" (p. 179), and on to 1914 when he confirms that.... "the banking lobby prevailed over common sense and over public interest; banks created money apace, and government created none. A more insane and shameful abnegation of government power is hardly imaginable". (p. 182)

THE CANADIAN EXPERIENCE

Writing in Glasgow in 1947, Thomas Robertson referred to a "remarkable piece of evidence" published in 1939 by the Canadian government. This evidence, to which we will revert, was in the form of extracts from the *Minutes of Proceedings and Evidence of the Standing Committee on Banking and Commerce*. This Committee had been set up because of the continuing "financial friction which has agitated the whole of Canada and has kept the political temperature high for the past twenty years". (12)

We shall see later that the political temperature in Canada is still high at the end of the twentieth century and that opposition to the dominance of private banking in the creation of Canada's money supply is increasingly effective.

Meanwhile, the political temperature and the continuing "financial friction" of which Robertson speaks was greatly heightened in the 1920s and early 1930s, as the Social Credit proposals of Major C. H. Douglas became widely discussed. This was especially true in Alberta, where the astonishing political victory of Aberhart's Social Credit party in August 1935 further raised the political temperature. It is for the moment enough to note that successive attempts to have Social Credit proposals implemented (especially in relation to control of Provincial credit by the Alberta government) were repeatedly subject to "violent attack by the financial powers-that-be in Canada, England, and the USA and several other countries" (13) and were blocked by the Federal Government in Ottawa.

And although a Social Credit government was returned to power in Alberta until the 1960s it never was allowed to implement Social Credit principles.

Today as a result, the "failure" of Social Credit is held up by its opponents as a warning to monetary reformers. And it is also remembered today, even by many monetary reformers in Canada, as having been the policy of a "right wing" movement!

Yet *Canada's Weekly* could sum up the position in an article published on March 26th 1948, by suggesting that "It is always said of the people of Alberta that they will "try anything once". But why do they vote for something that has been a "failure" – and vote for it not once but at three successive General Elections? It takes some explaining, doesn't it? The fact that they return a Social Credit Government again and again, with huge majorities, proves that they know Social Credit has not been tried and therefore has not failed. It proves also their stubborn determination to get what they voted for in 1935 – over twelve years ago." (14)

Meanwhile throughout Canada the Treasury Board continued to administer the 1923 Finance Act which left private banks free to decide "what cash they would obtain under the Act against their collateral security". (15) The economic results of this arrangement were increasingly unsatisfactory and in 1933 a Royal Commission recommended that a central bank be established. Parliament duly passed the Bank of Canada Act in 1934 and the following year the Bank was in operation.

To begin with all 12,000 shares were held privately, albeit each holder was limited to 50 shares. In 1938 however all outstanding shares in private hands were acquired by Government and from then the Bank has been owned by the federal government.

Continuing "financial friction" however led to the establishment of a Standing Committee on Banking and Commerce which took evidence from, amongst others, the Governor of the Bank, Mr. Graham F. Towers. In its Report published in 1939 the evidence given by Mr. Towers, largely under cross examination by Mr. G. McGreer K.C., was so remarkable for its time that Thomas Robertson felt compelled to quote it at some length. It remains such a powerful indictment of the current arrangements, which allow the dominance of private banks in the process of money creation, that it is worth rehearsing again some of the key parts of the evidence quoted by Robertson from the Committee's published minutes. (16) (emphasis added):

PURCHASE OF GOVERNMENT BONDS BY BANKS

Q. A banker can purchase a Dominion Government Bond by accepting from the Government, we will say, a Bond for $1,000 and giving to the Government a deposit in the bank for $1,000?
Mr. Towers: Yes.
Q. What the Government receives is a credit in the bankers book showing the banker as a debtor to the Goverment to the extent of $1,000?
Mr. Towers: Yes. (p. 76)

BOOK-KEEPING ENTRIES

Q. Ninety-five per cent of all our volume of business is being done with what we call exchange of bank deposits – **that is, simply book-keeping entries in banks against which people write cheques?**
Mr. Towers: I think that is a fair statement. (p. 233)

ISSUE OF CURRENCY

Q. Twelve per cent of the money in use in Canada is issued by the Government through the Mint and the Bank of Canada, and **88 per cent is issued by the merchant banks of Canada on reserves issued by the Bank of Canada?**
Mr. Towers: Yes.
Q. But if the issue of currency and money is a high prerogative of government, then the high prerogative has been transferred to the extent of 88 per cent, from the Government to the merchant banking system?
Mr. Towers: Yes. (p. 286)

CREATING NEW MONEY

Q. When a $1,000,000 worth of bonds is presented(by the government) to the bank **a million dollars of new money or the equivalent is created?**
Mr. Towers: Again assuming that there is no decrease in its other investments or loans.
Q. I mean at the time, at the moment.
Mr. Towers: Yes.
Q. Is it a fact that a million dollars of new money is created?
Mr. Towers: That is right. (p. 238)
Q. Now, the same thing holds true when the municipality or the province goes to the bank?
Mr. Towers: Or an individual borrower.
Q. Or a private person goes to a bank?
Mr. Towers: Yes.
Q. When I borrow $100 from the bank as a private citizen **the bank makes a book-keeping entry and there is $100 increase in the deposits of that bank, in the total deposits of that bank?**
Mr. Towers: Yes.

REPAYMENT OF BANK LOANS

Q. At the present time in Canada there is in the bank portfolios $1,400,000,000 in bonds?
Mr. Towers: Yes.
(Questions by Mr. Landeryou)
Q. If the government wished to pay off the bank loan – that is, retire this $1,400,000,000 – at the moment they would have to tax $1,400,000,000 away from the people; is that not right?
Mr. Towers: Yes.

Q. Now, we are going to tax the people because under the proposition I am trying to work out we are going to retire these bonds?
Mr. Towers: Yes.
Q. At the moment there is $2,500,000, 000 bank deposits?
Mr. Towers: Yes.
Q. And we are going to tax the people $1,400,000,000 to retire our bonds?
Mr. Towers: Yes... the government gives the banks a cheque
for $1,400,000,000 extinguishing the deposits and removing the bonds.

HOW MONEY DISAPPEARS

Q. What has happened to the $1,400,000,000 in the form of a cheque that comes to the bank?
Mr. Towers: The cheque is drawn on the government account in the bank.
Q. Is it cancelled by the bank?
Mr. Towers: Well, naturally.
Q. Well then, that much money goes out of existence?
Mr. Towers: Yes.

THE IRREDEEMABLE DEBT

(Questions by Mr. Dubuc) (p. 240)
Q. If the government by some means could tax the $1,400,000,000 so that they could buy the bonds that are in the hands of the bank, then the depositors would have to give a cheque out of their bank deposits to transfer it to the government and there would only remain $1,100,000,000 on deposit?
Mr. Towers: In the circumstances you mention... to visualize a sudden move of that kind, a sudden taxation in one year of an extra $1,400,000,000. is visualizing something which simply could not happen.
(Questions by Mr. Landeryou)
Q. It just could not happen because it would bankrupt the whole nation and destroy the assets of the people.
Mr. Towers: The transfer would dislocate the whole economic system.
Q. It would destroy everything?
Mr. Towers: Yes.

PAPER CURRENCY TO PURCHASE GOLD

Q. Now as a matter of fact today gold is purchased by the Bank of Canada with notes which it issues... not redeemable in gold... in effect using printing press money... to purchase gold?
Mr. Towers: That is the practice all over the world. (p. 283)

BANK ISSUE A SUBSTITUTE FOR MONEY

Q. When you allow the merchant banking system to issue deposits... with the practice of using cheques... you virtually allow the banks to issue an effective substitute for money, do you not?

Mr. Towers: The bank deposits are actually money in that sense.

Q. As a matter of fact they are **not actual money but credit, book-keeping accounts which are used as a substitute for money?**

Mr. Towers: **Yes.**

Q. Then we authorise the banks to issue a substitute for money?

Mr. Towers: Yes, I think that is a very fair statement of banking. (p. 285)

POWER TO CHANGE THE BANKING SYSTEM

Q. Will you tell me why a government with power to create money should give that power away to a private monopoly and then borrow that which parliament can create itself, back at interest, to the point of national bankruptcy?

Mr. Towers: We realise, of course, that the amount which is paid provides part of the operating costs of the banks and some interest on deposits. **Now if parliament wants to change the form of operating the banking system, then certainly that is within the power of parliament.** (p. 394)

INCREASE OF DEPOSITS AND INFLATION

Q. So that with the increase of $500 million of bank deposit money (from 1934 to 1938) we have not had any inflationary result?

Mr. Towers: We have not. The circumstances of the times have not encouraged it. (p. 643)

FINANCE IN WAR AND PEACE

Q. So far as war is concerned, to defend the integrity of the nation there will be no difficulty in raising the means of financing whatever those requirements may be?

Mr. Towers: The limit of the possibilities depends upon men and materials.

Q. **And where you have an abundance of men and materials you have no difficulty, under our present banking system, of putting forth the medium of exchange that is necessary to put the men and materials to work in defence of the realm?**

Mr. Towers: **That is right.**

Q. **Well then, why is it, where we have a problem of internal deterioration, that we cannot use the same technique...** in any event you will agree with me on this, that so long as the investment of public funds is confined to something that improves the economic life of the nation, that will not of itself produce an inflationary result.

Mr. Towers: Yes, I agree with that, but I shall make one further qualification, that the investment thus made shall be at least as productive as some alternative uses to which the money would otherwise be put. (p. 649)

GOVERNMENT EXPENDITURE DIRECTLY RECOVERED

Q. You do not suggest that it is necessary that the government should be able to recover the money that it invests in capital works, providing those works are beneficial to the country?
Mr. Towers: The Government indirectly really does recover, because what benefits the country will benefit the Government, and the Government revenue, even though you cannot see that this specific thing has done it. (p. 768)

PHYSICALLY POSSIBLE AND FINANCIALLY POSSIBLE

Q. **Would you admit that anything physically possible and desirable can be made financially possible?**
Mr. Towers: **Certainly.**

Throughout so much of that evidence it is possible to see the tremendous influence of the work of C. H. Douglas. The last question and answer is an especially powerful reflection of the essence of his position. It is also a total repudiation of the position of most governments and economists then and now. Indeed since the late 1970s the cry of "Where is the money to come from?" has probably never been louder.

In this atmosphere of "financial friction" which was agitating Canada in those years, it probably seemed quite natural to most Canadians that the Bank of Canada should in fact create "most of the nation's money supply from 1935 to 1939 and 62% of new money during the last years of World War II... [which as a result]... gave Canada the highest employment rate it has ever had, very low interest rates, and very low inflation". (17)

Alas, after the war the percentage of Canada's money supply produced by the Bank of Canada began to decline. Eventually, under very different direction from that of Mr. Towers, it responded enthusiastically to the monetarist agenda promoted via the Bank for International Settlements in the 1970s, and the decline accelerated. By 1992 the percentage of Canada's money supply created by the Bank of Canada had dropped to barely 7.5%.

Throughout the history of unremitting opposition to the debt-money system there have been a small number of extraordinary individuals who have understood the system well. Many of them could not only identify the root cause of recurring crises, but were also prepared to argue openly, and at considerable personal cost, for its radical reform.

A short introductory note on one or two of the more prominent amongst them may be useful before we look in a bit more detail at their specific proposals.

C. H. DOUGLAS

Foremost amongst these critics for a while was Major C. H. Douglas. The collapse of the international financial system in 1929, and its devastating social impact, had in fact been forecast by him with astonishing accuracy nearly a decade earlier. He was a consulting engineer who had worked in a senior capacity with the Canadian General Electric Company; as Deputy Chief Electrical Engineer with the Buenos Aires and Pacific Railway and as Chief Engineer and Manager in India for the British Westinghouse Company. Before the outbreak of war in 1914 he was involved in conducting early work on the Post Office Tube in London and later supervised the installation of plant in "one of the earliest examples of complete automation in the history of engineering". (18)

From service in the war as a major in the Royal Flying Corps he was sent in 1916 to the Farnborough Aircraft Establishment to try to resolve difficulties with the factory accounts. It was during this work that he recognised that the factory was generating costs faster than it was distributing incomes in the form of wages and salaries.

If this were true for the economy as a whole, the implication was that it would be impossible in any production period to buy with the purchasing power of wages, salaries and dividends alone, the whole product of the economy at prices which included total input costs. The result would be a shortage of consumer purchasing power and a corresponding gathering of surplus goods of all kinds. These might be temporarily disposed of by export in excess of imports, sale below cost as in bankruptcy, waste or by further borrowing by consumers or entrepreneurs. Borrowing by consumers however would have to be repaid out of future income and the result would be an even greater deficiency of purchasing power in the next period. Wages, salaries and dividends distributed by entrepreneurs in the course of a new round of production, **in advance of the related goods and services being available for sale**, would also help to clear the current surplus. However when the goods resulting from this new round of production were marketed, an even greater shortage of purchasing power would become evident as businesses and consumers were required to repay to the banks the sums borrowed plus interest!

Whatever the interim solution, the end result would always eventually be surpluses accruing on an unmanagable scale, leading first to trade wars to "capture export markets" and finally to the "logical and inevitable end of economic competition" (19), military war. This hypothesis certainly seemed to fit the facts of centuries of previous experience and is supported by Robert Lekachman who notes perceptively in his *The Age of Keynes* that "The war pointed a sharp Keynesian moral. As a public works project, all wars (before the nuclear era) are ideal. **Since all war production is sheer economic waste, there never is a danger of producing too much... In the world of 1941-5, what occurred was full employment, bustling factories and an increase in the production of useful as well as useless things. In real life these were the consequences of waste... and in World War II... the equivalent of the Egyptian pyramids, the medieval cathedrals, and the buried bottles full of money were the tanks, the bombers and the aircraft carriers.**" (20) (emphasis added)

Douglas meanwhile collected information on 100 major companies in Britain and found that, except in some cases where businesses were approaching bankruptcy, total costs were in fact always greater than total purchasing power released in the form of wages, salaries and dividends.

He was thus stimulated to bring his professional engineer's approach to a detailed analysis of the financial/economic system and its inevitable economic and social consequencies.

He concluded that the primary reform, **without which no solution of the economic problem was possible**, was that the power to create a nation's money supply must revert to the State, albeit with suitable technical and democratic safeguards to avoid politically motivated abuse.

He also argued for two other key elements of reform – the National Dividend and a mechanism which would produce a Scientific or Just Price for goods and services and act as a double lock against inflation.

These ideas were explained in a series of books, essays and speeches, and the rest of his life was spent struggling for radical reform, against determined and immensely powerful opposition.

The Wall Street Crash and the ensuing international economic crisis had powerfully confirmed his diagnosis and gave him a world-wide reputation. He was invited to make speaking tours of Canada, Australia and New Zealand.

He addressed the World Engineering Congress in Tokyo in 1929 and in 1935 addressed an important gathering of the Oslo Merchants'Club at which both the Norwegian King and the British Minister were present. He was invited to give evidence to the Canadian Banking Enquiry of 1923 and to the Macmillan Committee in London in 1930.

However his analysis and prescriptions for change were vigorously opposed by financiers, most orthodox economists and quite importantly by senior figures(notably Sydney and Beatrice Webb)in the Labour Party, despite great interest at that time within the socialist movement especially in Scotland.

By the time preparations had begun for war in the second half of the 1930s, and with the publication of Keynes's *General Theory of Employment, Interest, and Money* which could be accommodated to financial and economic orthodoxy, Douglas's ideas were no longer referred to in the media and lost much of their currency. Douglas himself was damned with faint praise by Keynes and was categorised by many orthodox economists as a "crank".

Athough Douglas was probably the most high profile critic of the debt-money system during those years, he was by no means alone.

FREDERICK SODDY

Frederick Soddy was another extraordinary individual who, from outside the academic speciality of economics, brought startling new insight to its study and unequivocally identified the debt-money system as the root cause of the economic problem. He was an internationally respected researcher in the study of the chemistry of radio-active materials. He worked with Rutherford trying to unlock the secrets of atomic power and became a Professor of Chemistry at Oxford University. In 1922 he was awarded the Nobel Prize in chemistry.

He was appalled at the way in which science could be exploited for the Great War but not for peace and prosperity after it. He noted that "Year after year the industrialised nations produced an ever mounting tide of munitions for war, with the flower of their manhood withdrawn from production... whereas now we have returned to peace and squalor, to idle factories... we are back as a nation to pre-war conditions... with a million and a quarter workers unemployed, unable to feed and clothe ourselves adequately and unable even to build houses in which to live under the existing economic system". (21) .

As he examined the financial/economic system he claimed that economists had confused debt which is a claim on wealth, for wealth itself. They were therefore in a hopeless tangle, counting money as an asset, i.e. real wealth, when in fact it is a liability – an obligation of the community to provide wealth on demand.

An important result of this he suggested is that "those who create and deal in money can receive rewards from the economic system as generous as if the money they had invented by the process of banking had been real wealth created by the same sort of human effort as is required, for instance, for the mining of gold.". (22)

He was convinced that the threatened collapse of our Western civilisation was not a consequence of political philosophies or antagonisms. Instead it followed from the application of the defective money system which ensured eventual collapse and that meanwhile en route, we should "lead a harried, driven life, concerned for the most part with the immediate necessity of keeping the wolf from the door, and destroying our trade rivals.". (23)

Alas Soddy too, despite his brilliant academic career and the rigour of his challenge, was subjected to the ire of those whom he challenged and duly accorded the reputation of crank.

HENRY FORD AND THOMAS A. EDISON

In America meanwhile savage criticism was coming from a quite different quarter. Two major figures from the world of practical capitalism, Henry Ford and Thomas Edison visited the giant unfinished dam on the Tennessee River near Muscle Shoals, Alabama, and offered interesting proposals for funding its completion. These proposals were discussed in the *New York Times* of December 4th and 6th 1921 and by William Hixson in one of his contributions to *The COMER Papers* (24) which includes the following extracts:

> Army engineers say that it will take $40,000,000 to complete the big [Muscle Shoals] dam. But Congress is economical just now and not in a mood to raise the money by taxation. The customary alternative is thirty-year bonds at 4 per cent. The United States, the greatest Government in the world, wishing $40,000,000 to complete a great public benefit is forced to go to the money sellers... At the end of thirty years the Government not only has to pay back the $40,000,000, but it has to pay 120 per cent interest, literally has to pay $88,000,000 for the use of $40,000,000 for thirty years... Think of it. Could anything be more... unbusinesslike?
>
> Now I see a way by which our Government can get this great work completed without paying a nickel to the money sellers. It is a way as sound as granite. .
> The Government needs $40,000,000. That is 2,000,000 twenty-dollar bills. Let the Government issue those bills and with them pay every expense connected with the completion of the dam.

What is there behind a bond... that makes it acceptable? Simply the good faith and credit of the American people, and twenty-dollar bills issued by Government to complete this great public improvement would have just as much of the good faith and credit of the American people behind them as any bond... Whenever the Government needs money for a great public improvement, instead of thinking of bonds with heavy interest, think of... currency. Do you really see what the interest charges of our Government mount up to?

The national debt is nothing more or less than the nation's interest liability pile. Every public improvement this country makes means an increase in the national debt. But here is a way to get improvements without increasing the debt... The only difference between the currency plan and the bond plan is that there is no interest to be paid, and the Wall Street money merchants, who do nothing to build the dam and deserve nothing, will get nothing.

(H. Ford, New York Times December 4th 1921)

Now here is Ford proposing to finance Muscle Shoals by an issue of currency. Very well, let us suppose for a moment that Congress will follow his proposal.

Personally I do not think Congress has the imagination to do it, but let us suppose that it does. The required sum is authorized... The bills are issued directly by Government as all money ought to be. When workmen are paid off they receive these United States bills. When the material is bought it is paid in these United States bills.

Question: But suppose Congress does not agree to this. What then?

Answer: Well Congress must fall back on the old way of doing business. It must authorize the issue of bonds. That is, it must go out to the money brokers and borrow... and we must pay interest to the money brokers... That is to say, under the old way any time we wish to add to the national wealth we must add to the national debt. Now that is what Henry Ford wants to prevent. He thinks it is stupid and so do I...

People who will not turn a shovelful of dirt nor contribute a pound of material will collect more money from the United States than the people who do the work. That is the terrible thing about interest. In all our great bond issues the interest is always greater than the principal. All the great public works cost more than twice the actual cost on that account... But here is the point: If our nation can issue a dollar bond it can issue a dollar bill. The element that makes the bond good makes the bill good also.

The difference between the bond and the bill is that the bond lets the money brokers collect twice the amount of the bond and an additional 20 per cent whereas the currency pays nobody but those who directly contribute to Muscle Shoals in some useful way.

If the Government issues bonds, it simply induces the money brokers to draw dollars out of other channels of trade and turn it into Muscle Shoals; if Government issues currency, it provides itself with enough money to increase the national wealth at Muscles Shoals without disturbing the business of the rest of the country. And in doing this it increases its income without adding a penny to its debt.

It is absurd to say that our country can issue millions of dollars in bonds but not in currency...

[But one way] fattens the usurer, and the other helps the people. If the currency issued by Government were no good, then bonds issued would be no good either. It is a terrible situation when the Government, to increase the national wealth, must go into debt and submit to ruinous interest... If the United States Government will adopt this policy of increasing its national wealth without contributing to the interest collector – for the whole of the national debt is made up of interest charges – then you will see an era of progress and prosperity in this country such as could never have come otherwise.

(Attributed to Edison in an article in *New York Times* December 6th 1921)

It is worth recalling from our earlier argument that while Edison's analysis is essentially accurate, he omits an important point when he says that "If Government issues bonds, it simply induces money brokers to withdraw dollars out of other channels of trade". In fact banks may buy government bonds with money they create "out of nothing" simply by drawing a cheque against themselves and still simultaneously lend money to fund private enterprises up to the limit of their notion of "prudent lending" if indeed they can find the borrowers.

Henry Ford and Thomas Edison made their criticisms of the debt-money system in the specific context of the major public works represented by the Muscle Shoal dam. On the other hand, Soddy and especially Douglas, were attacking the foundations of the debt-money system throughout the 1920s well before the crash on Wall Street and on into the 1930s. However as the depression deepened in the early 1930s powerful criticism also began to come from within the economics profession itself.

Almost simultaneously John Maynard Keynes in Britain, and Professors Irving Fisher and Henry Simons in America launched major critiques of the system and set out detailed proposals for change.

Both Fisher and Simons developed their proposals on the principle that money creation should become the sole prerogative of the state. Keynes however, although clearly aware of the operation and impact of the existing system of money creation by banks, chose not to attack it directly.

J. M. KEYNES

John Maynard Keynes was born into a prosperous Cambridge family in 1883. His parents were both graduates of Cambridge University and the family is described as living in "moderate circumstances but solid comfort... [which implied however]... an ample domestic staff, travel in Europe, theatre and concert going, books and periodicals in quantity, and naturally the very best of schools and universities for the children of the home". (25)

He was an outstanding student at Eton and at King's College Cambridge. He showed considerable aptitude for economics and was encouraged to decide on a professional career in economics by such illustrious figures as Alfred Marshall and A. C. Pigou. Instead he sat the civil service examinations hoping to enter the

Treasury. He came second in the exams however and chose a job at the India Office. He was appointed in 1913 to the Royal Commission on Indian Currency and Finance and met a number of prominent people who were later to be important to his career. From his days at Cambridge he was acquainted with Lytton Strachey and later became a member of the group of highly influential men and women who formed the Bloomsbury Group. Eventually he did realise his original ambition when he was summoned to the Treasury in 1915 to work with Sir George Paish, Advisor to the Chancellor of the Exchequer, and to the Treasury on Financial and Economic affairs. By 1918 he had attained the rank of Assistant Secretary and was third in rank at the Treasury. Meanwhile he had been made a CB (Companion of the Bath) and in 1919 went, with great positive effect on his reputation, as financial representative to the Paris Peace Conference. In 1929 he was made a member of the highly prestigious Macmillan Committee set up to enquire into banking, finance and credit. Amongst those who appeared before it was one of his principal teachers at Cambridge A. C. Pigou, his friend D. H. Robertson and Major C. H. Douglas.

In 1936 he published his *General Theory of Employment, Interest and Money* which provided the basis in due course for the development of a new Keynesian school of economic thought.

Although it seemed a radical departure from the current orthodoxy, and attempts were made by his friends, notably R. G. Hawtrey and D. H. Robertson to dissuade him from such a significant attack on classical economics, it was not too long before his ideas were accommodated within the orthodox paradigm. A key insight, which Keynes arrived at in detailed discussion with D. H. Robertson, was that Say's Law was fatally flawed. Say's Law insisted that "Supply creates its own demand" so that any increases in output would automatically generate a balancing increase in demand. In its later form it had been strengthened by the suggestion that adjustments in interest rates would ensure similar equilibrium between savings and investment.

All income would therefore be spent either on consumption or investment goods and all resources would be used. The result was that full employment would be the natural condition of the economy. If however full employment did not obtain at some time, its absence would be because of accident, monopoly action by business or trade unions or inappropriate government policies. Keynes and Robertson on the other hand believed that some savings might not in fact be utilised in investment. If this were so, the automatic mechanisms implied in Say's Law would not operate to produce full employment and public intervention would be necessary.

In fact when their analysis and prescription for public works was published as a key proposition in *The General Theory*, it was said to confirm the merit in Lloyd George's call for public works in 1904 so that "Robertson and Keynes finally brought their profession up to the level of political instinct". (26) It could also be said that they had similarly accepted Major Douglas's proposition that cyclical recessions and periodic depressions were caused by a recurring shortfall in aggregate demand.

There was a great deal more of course in *The General Theory* which represented a repudiation of much of the Classical position. However, although

Keynes must clearly have been very well aware of how the banking system was operated, and did indeed advocate the "euthenasia of the rentier", there was nothing about the kind of need for radical change to that system which Douglas had proposed to the Macmillan Committee.

It may indeed be, that as Keynes recognized that it would be extremely difficult to get governments to commit themselves to sensible expansionary expenditures, he decided not to make it even harder by suggesting that they also should create the necessary money "out of thin air". The matter after all was of the greatest importance and "since the public was, and still is, largely ignorant of the fact that private bankers do exactly this when they approve loans, his evasion of the issue was probably wise salesmanship". (27)

We have already noted that the Keynesian analysis and prescription was widely applied and seemed to be hugely successful from the late thirties, when there was huge public investment in armaments and other work related to the preparations for war, until the early 1970s.

Then however, the simultaneous appearance of inflation and unemployment, aggravated by two major oil crises and gathering international indebtedness finally brought the Keynesian consensus to an end. It simply could not be successful, on any long term basis, while it failed to include radical reform of the banking system.

IRVING FISHER AND HENRY C. SIMONS

And yet at virtually the same time as Keynes was developing the ideas which were presented in *The General Theory*, across the Atlantic a number of economists, including the major figures of Irving Fisher and Henry Simons, were disputing at least some of the key propositions of Keynes and promoting a much more radical program for change. Fisher for example was highly dubious about the importance of "over-production, under-consumption, over-capacity... over-confidence... over-saving... and the discrepancy between saving and investment" to any adequate explanation of business cycles. Instead he advanced the opinion that in the great booms and depressions, each of these played a "subordinate role as compared with... overindebtedness... In short the big bad actors are debt disturbances and price level-disturbances [due to money supply disturbances]". (28)

Irving Fisher was Professor of Economics at Yale University and Simons was Professor of Economics at Chicago during this time and both were severe critics of fractional reserve banking. At the centre of their proposals there was an unambiguous recognition of the fact that "The major proximate factor in the present crisis is commercial banking". (29)

If the causes of recurring crises were to be solved therefore their view was that the current banking system must be reformed, and the first step must be to withdraw from commercial banks their existing power to create "out of nothing" the bulk of the nation's money supply.

Their ideas, in many respects close to those of Douglas and Soddy, were outlined in considerable detail in Fisher's *100% Money* published in 1935, and Simons's *Economic Policy for a Free Society* published posthumously in 1948 just two years after he died at the age of 47.

It was the Keynesian program however, rather than the ideas of Douglas, Soddy, Fisher and Simons, which triumphed and were pursued with increasing commitment and confidence by most of the industrial world until the early 1970s and the onset of the current, and most serious depression the world has yet faced.

No wonder John Hotson (30), Professor of Economics at Waterloo University until his retirement, was to lament in his introduction to Hixson's *A Matter of Interest* that when Keynes was pressed about the likely long-term impact of increasing government debts, he was wont simply to offer a sharp retort to the effect that "In the long run we are all dead!" Hotson again allows however that "given the clear and present danger to civilisation posed by totalitarian fascism and communism in the 1930s who can fault him for taking this view?".

Yet he also notes that "the long run is upon us and the results of following Keynes(and Hitler) rather than Fisher and Simons out of the Great Depression have been tragic. The world is now faced with national and international overindebtedness crises that have slowed progress in the developed world and plunged the poor nations of Africa and Latin America into a depression more cruel and longer lived already than the Great Depression of the 1930s. Who can say whether the worst is over or not yet begun?"

If we consider only the continuing deterioration in the global environment it must be clear that in fact the worst is far from over. It cannot, and will not be over until there has been widespread recognition of the pernicious role played by the debt-money system and action to change it has been taken. It is time now therefore, to look first at some of the detailed proposals of these would-be reformers and then to construct an action plan to ensure that recognition and change.

Notes

1. Robertson T.   1975 p. 105
2. Robertson T.   1975 p. 107
3. De Màre E.   1986 p. 96/97
4. Robertson T.   1975 p. 157
5. Born K. E.   1976 p. 7
6. Born K. E.   1976 p. 9
7. Born K. E.   1976 p. 273
8. Krehm W.   1993 p. 3
9. Grubiak O. J.   1988 p. 8
10. Grubiak O. J.   1988 p. 8
11. Grubiak O. J.   1988 p. 11
12. Robertson T.   1975 p. 71
13. Douglas C. H.   1984 p. xxiii
14. Hargreaves J.   1948
15. Krehm W.   1993 p. 2
16. Robertson T.   1975 p. 71/78
17. Chorney H. et al.   1992 p. 9
18. Douglas C. H.   1979 p. 180
19. Douglas C. H.   1974 p. 137
20. Lekachman R.   1966 p. 130
21. Soddy F.   1926 p. 21
22. Hattersley J. M.   1988 p. 193
23. Soddy F.   1926 p. 65
24. Hixson W.   1992 p. 54/58
25. Lekachman R.   1966 p. 13
26. Lekachman R.   1966 p. 59
27. Hixson W.   1991 p. xxi
28. Hixson W.   1991 p. 99
29. Simons H.   1948 p. 54
30. Hixson W.   1991 p. xxii

CHAPTER
8

SOME DETAILED PROPOSALS FOR CHANGE

That the world's financial/economic system is in crisis will be readily acknowledged by the great majority of the world's peoples. After all, the major problems that result from this crisis – global environmental damage, mass unemployment and poverty, stress and social breakdown – are all too evident to the millions who suffer from them.

Many fewer people however are confident that politicians, financial experts or orthodox economists can, or are willing to offer any accurate analysis of the causes of the crisis, far less prescribe any **effective** remedy. Meanwhile everything in the orthodox repertoire it seems, has been tried and found wanting.

In principle it may be widely accepted that the system needs radical reforms of a kind which are not currently contemplated by the orthodox. But what could be the nature of the necessary radical measures and how might they be put into practice?

Many of the people who have agitated for radical change to the system, have concentrated largely on the proposition that control of money creation should reside with the State and not with private banks. Others however have looked more closely at the mechanics of change and worked out more comprehensive proposals for the system as a whole. Some have also seen the need for fundamental changes to the democratic system to accompany radical change to the debt-money system, and yet others argue for a change in the objectives of economic activity itself.

We shall deal here with the major financial/economic proposals of just a few of the most frequently discussed advocates of radical change. But in constructing our strategy for change in the next chapter, some of the other ideas will be referred to.

MAJOR C. H. DOUGLAS

At the core of Douglas's analysis was his criticism of the international debt-money system – the way credit (money) creation was operated as a monopoly by commercial bankers. He maintained that the economic system could not be sustained in the long run under this arrangement. The key features of its progress to eventual collapse he identified as endemic inflation, a frenzy of "super production", economic and military wars in pursuit of foreign markets, waste, degradation of the environment and an inexorable rise in unemployment resulting from technical progress. On the other hand he insisted that unemployment should be seen as a sign of economic progress rather than as a symptom of economic breakdown and his proposals show how this might be the case.

He was also an advocate of radical change to the mechanics of the democratic process.

In his proposals for economic change however there are three key propositions:

MONEY CREATION

Creation of the nation's money supply by commercial banks should be discontinued. Money should instead be created by a statutory authority but with safeguards against any prospect of its manipulation for party political purposes.

It might be issued by a National Credit Office (NCO) which would be insulated from day-to-day interference by government. Its central function will be to establish in each accountancy period, the total prices of finished goods in the economy and the corresponding total purchasing power available to consumers. For the reasons outlined previously there will almost always be a gap between the two which can be established with reasonable accuracy by procedures similar to those currently employed by the Central Statistical Office. Athough the total amount of money to be newly created in each period would be strictly controlled, the NCO would reflect government input at this stage, and issue purchasing power to consumers in any, or all of three ways to bridge this gap. It should be noted that NCO creation of money would be no more inflationary than similar sums created by banks would be. In fact because there would be little or no interest involved, and because the amount issued would be **tightly related to the economy's physical capacity to produce goods and services, there would be virtually no tendency to inflation at all**.

The NCO may issue part of the annual creation of money to meet the costs of government commissioned work on the nation's infrastructure and public services. The balance then would be issued in the forms of a National Dividend and as credits to producers and/or retailers in connection with the maintenance of an inflation-free economy through the mechanism of the "Scientific Price".

THE SCIENTIFIC OR JUST PRICE

Douglas denied the generally held view that the retail price of goods could never, economically, be less than the financial cost of their production. Certainly under the current financial system it had to be accepted that if a producer paid £100 for raw materials and a further £150 for wages and overhead charges then the price of his output could not, economically, be less than £250. But if the system were based on the real credit of the community rather than on the "so called gold basis" then this need not hold.

By way of illustration, C. M. Hattersley, (1) who was an influential supporter of the Douglas analysis, developed this part of the Douglas argument broadly as follows:

Assume that in a given time, the gross increase in the real credit of the community, i.e. not just output but the increased capacity of the community to produce, is £1 million. Simultaneously gross decrease in real credit i.e., consumption of goods plus depreciation and scrapping of plant, is £800,000.

Clearly therefore in the given time period there has been a nett appreciation of the community's real credit to the value of £200,000. This nett increase in real credit under the proposed system would provide backing for a Treasury issue of new financial credit of not more than £200,000.

Now suppose that the price of goods within the community were regulated at 4/5ths of production costs. Then when the goods costing £800,000 had been sold, manufacturers would be out of pocket by £160,000 and this could be re-imbursed to them by means of a Treasury issue of new financial credit. If therefore in a given period gross production of community real credit be represented by 10 and simultaneously gross consumption by 8 then nett appreciation of communal real credit is represented by 2.

Total real benefit received by individual consumers represents real credit absorbed 8 and total real benefit to the community as a whole represents the nett increase in real credit 2.

Under the given conditons therefore any price paid to producers for their commodities (i.e. production cost plus profit) should be borne as to 8 parts by individual consumers and 2 parts by the community as a whole, i.e. 8/10ths of the selling price is borne by consumers and 2/10ths is credited to producers by the Treasury on behalf of the community as a whole.

So with a financial system based on real credit the Just or Scientific Price of a good to the consumer, bears to the cost of its production the same ratio as does the Gross Depreciation of Communal Real Credit bear to its Gross Appreciation.

So that:
$$\frac{\text{Scientific Price}}{\text{Cost Price}} = \frac{\text{Cons. of Real Credit}}{\text{Prod. of Real Credit}} = \text{P. Factor}$$

The retail price of each product produced becomes its cost of production plus profit multiplied by the price factor for the period and in Mr. Hattersley's example that would be 80%.

Application of the Price Factor in practice may be likened to the application of a negative Value Added Tax and would operate without undermining the role of price as a market signal.

Douglas insisted that the Scientific Price would ensure that inflation could not occur because:

a. NCO issue of new money would simply represent in money terms the real expansion in the capacity of the community to deliver goods and services since the last credit issue.

b. Those issues which would be credits in respect of maintaining the Scientific Price would be the means of reducing prices to consumers to below their cost of production.

THE NATIONAL DIVIDEND

The National Dividend is designed to make concrete Douglas's proposal that each individual member of the community should have, as of right, some equitable share of the community's wealth in the form of goods and services. It also allows that the inevitability of "unemployment" might be seen by most people as representing progress to a prosperous and spiritually satisfying leisured society.

If unemployment, in relation to paid work, must inevitably increase as technical progress continues, then there will have to be an alternative arrangement for distributing purchasing power to consumers. If there is not, then it will be to an increasing extent impossible for the product of the economy to be consumed. Douglas suggested therefore that the logical and natural partner of the wage system is a system of dividends which are distributed to individual members of the community quite independently of their remuneration from paid work, or from any other "external consideration".

In anticipation of criticism of his proposal on "moral" grounds – i.e. that the dividend would represent something for nothing, he emphasised what he called the Cultural Inheritance of the Community. By this he meant the capital gifts of nature; the benefits of scientific and technological innovation; ordered government; industrial, social and political organisation; education, religion and a hundred and one amenities of civilisation which each generation had passed to it by countless previous generations of mankind.

This proposal therefore involves each individual member of the community receiving, as a matter of right, a dividend representing a proper share in the increase, from period to period, in the real credit of the community as a whole. It would be received whether the individual were employed or not and without regard to financial status. The dividend would be financed from the increasing real credit of the community so that as the community's productive capacity increased, the dividend would rise. While it was to be paid as part of the individual's birthright and not as a dole, it was not to be raised by taxes or national insurance contributions.

It would be, like producer credits in respect of the Scientific Price, paid from newly created credits issued by the NCO. With rising productivity the National Dividend would in due course replace all unemployment benefits, family allowances, income support and other social benefits, and as it rose would tend to replace wages and salaries. Taxation would rapidly be reduced and perhaps eventually eliminated.

So via Douglas's proposals for the NCO; the Scientific Price and the National Dividend, the private monopoly of credit would be eliminated and control of credit would revert to "Crown, Parliament and People, and could be adjusted realistically, justly, and democratically for the well-being of the individual". (2) Unemployment as we know it would then have the potential to confer great blessings on humanity rather than being the curse that most of us consider it to be today.

It is interesting to note here that a recent academic review of Douglas's proposals for a National Dividend (promoted enthusiastically at the time by A. R. Orage, editor of *The New Age*) concluded that "The Douglas/Orage critique of capitalist finance as presented in the 1920s is highly relevant to contemporary concerns. Selectivity and targetting of benefits inhibits participation in paid employment for recipients while placing an increasing burden of transfer payments in the form of taxation and National Insurance contributions on employers and employees. **Attempts to ameliorate the system may prove less fruitful than radical restructuring in line with the Douglas/Orage analysis**". (3) (emphasis added)

FREDERICK SODDY

Soddy (4) recognises two forms of "wealth", real or absolute wealth and virtual wealth. The former is based on the nature of "physical or material wealth, in the sense of the physical requisites which empower and enable human life". Virtual wealth on the other hand is the "power conferred on individuals by the monetary system not to possess but to be owed wealth to which they are entitled, in order that any kind or quantity desired may be obtained as and when required without effort".

He makes therefore a major distinction in the subject matter of economics between that which is physical i.e. **wealth** and that which is psychological i.e. **debt**. In the process he maintained that this distinction brought to the study of economics "the most astonishing simplification" that provided the basis on which economics might at last become a science.

It would remain then only for "intellectual fearlessness and honesty to face things as they are and not as they appear... to abolish poverty and economic degradation from our midst in less time than it took the War to run its course". (5)

His practical conclusions about the nature of the system and proposals for the resolution of the financial/economic problem are summarised in the last chapter of his book and the following rehearses the substance of just some of his key points. (6) (emphasis added)

a. The production of Wealth, as distinct from Debt, obeys the physical laws of conservation and the exact reasoning of the physical sciences can be applied. The scale on which wealth can be produced is practically limited only by the state of technical knowledge of the time. There is therefore no longer any valid physical justification for the continuance of poverty.

b. Money, as a claim on real wealth, is now a form of national debt, owned by the individual or institutions and owed by the community and exchangeable for wealth by transference to another individual or institution.

c. Banks create and destroy money arbitrarily and with no understanding of the laws that correlate its quantity with national income (real wealth). They have been allowed to regard themselves as the owners of the virtual wealth which the community does **not** possess, and they lend it and charge interest on the loan as though it really existed and they possessed it. The wealth so acquired by the impecunious borrower is not given up by the lenders (who receive interest on the loan but give up nothing), but is given up by the whole community, who suffer in consequence the loss through a general reduction of purchasing power of money.

d. The banks have usurped the "Prerogative of the Crown" with regard to the issue of money and have corrupted the purpose of money from an exchange medium to that of an interest-bearing debt. These powers have fallen to them in consequence of the invention and development of the cheque system. It has been connived at by politicians of all parties, and in the process **they have abdicated the most important function of government and ceased to be de facto rulers of the nation.** The issue and withdrawal of money therefore should be restored to the nation for the general good and it should cease from providing a source of livelihood to private corporations. It should not bear interest because of its existence, but only when genuinely lent by an owner who **gives it up** to the borrower.

e. The issue of money should be regulated so that its purchasing power remains constant, more being issued if the purchasing power tends to rise or the price index tends to fall, and some withdrawn from circulation if purchasing power tends to fall and the general price level to rise. The money issued should defray national expenditure in lieu of taxation or redeem interest bearing National debt. The withdrawal of money should be by taxation or raising a National loan.

f. To initiate the system some £2 billion of National interest-bearing Debt should be cancelled and the same sum of national money (non interest-bearing National Debt) issued to replace the credit created by banks. The taxpayers would thereby be relieved of the payment of £100,000,000 a year interest on purely fictitious loans.

g. The banks should by law be required to keep national money £ for £ of their liabilities for customers'deposits in current account. They should be permitted to lend only money that has been genuinely deposited into their keeping by its owners, who give up the use of it for the stipulated period of the loan.

h. Credit should be issued, not cancelled, when supplies outrun demand (as a result of technical progress).

i. Taxation, as hitherto confined to the purpose of defraying government expenditure, is entirely futile as an instrument of permanent social amelioration, and should be used in conjunction with the issue of government loans for specific purposes such as building the country's infrastructure and more generally, for more actively influencing the proper development of the country, on the information supplied by the national statistical authority.

IRVING FISHER

In the early 1930s Irving Fisher was described by Joseph Schumpeter as America's "greatest scientific economist". In 1932 he wrote an analysis of the Great Depression in *Booms and Depressions,* and in 1935 he followed that analysis with detailed proposals for restructuring the economy in his book *100% Money.*

Unfortunately there appears to be no copy of this latter important book now available within the UK or European Library systems.

Once again therefore we must turn to Hixson (7), this time to his *A Matter of Interest* and to COMER for a review of his proposals for monetary and economic reform. Hixson notes that the single most important element of the necessary restructuring of the economy is the implementation of "The 100% Reserve Plan, which was devised and championed by... Henry Simons and Irving Fisher".

This plan would involve abolishing the current fractional reserve banking system. Instead it would require that in respect of a bank deposit against which a depositor might demand cash or write cheques the bank must maintain 100% reserves in legal tender money, i.e. notes and coins produced by government fiat.

The plan was not to involve the nationalisation of banks. Fisher was concerned rather to "nationalise money, not to nationalise banking". He envisages in fact the re-organisation of the banking system so that individual banks would have three completely separate departments, or that they would be replaced by three independent financial institutions, of which **none would be allowed to create money.** (8) (emphasis added)

The three new bank departments or new institutions would be:

CHEQUEING BANKS which would have a role in administering individual current accounts against which their clients may draw cheques in the usual way. Bank remuneration would be by charging for administration of the accounts. There would always be cash/legal tender money in the bank to meet any withdrawal by clients either directly or by cheque payment to another party.

MORTGAGE-LOAN INSTITUTIONS to serve the needs of small businesses and home owners. These institutions or bank departments would be required to hold in cash only a fraction of time deposits. They would pay interest on deposits and make secured loans at higher rates than those paid to depositors. They would therefore be financial intermediaries, operating in the way that banks are currently widely understood to operate.

INVESTMENT TRUSTS whose role would be to assist in the financing of corporate and large businesses. They would obtain funds only by selling equity shares on the open market and they would pay dividends (if any) on the basis of dividends received from the ownership of equity shares in non-financial companies or from interest received from making long term non-callable loans to businesses. They would be required to give preference to the purchase of new issue equities and to making business loans primarily of a job creating nature. They would be required to keep most of their assets in equity shares rather than in "debt paper".

These last two organisations would be prohibited from making loans for the purchase of equity, commodity trading, leveraged buyouts or any generally speculative purpose.

All speculative trading would therefore need 100% cash or would need interpersonal loans in cash.

Fisher then outlined in detail how the transition to the 100% reserve system would be arranged. Government would create a "Currency Commission" and through that mechanism, there would be issued enough money to purchase the real assets of each bank, or to lend it on the security of these real assets, so as to increase their cash reserves to a level equal to 100% of their "checking deposits" (sic). The banks thereafter "would be required to maintain permanently a cash reserve of 100% against its demand deposits". Banks would then be given a reasonable time to repay the money advanced by government and they would do this by liquidating all loans and investments, with the proceeds being passed to government.

Once the 100% Reserve Plan was effected, government would ensure price stability by increasing the money supply to allow for such annual level of economic growth as is physically possible, and presumably subject only to it being also desirable.

HENRY C. SIMONS

One of Simons's early essays *A Positive Program for Laissez Faire* first published in 1934, and included in *Economic Policy for a Free Society*, identified him as "a disciple of the great nineteenth-century tradition... [while at the same time separating him]... from the horde of reactionaries who mistakenly assume that this tradition is wholly negative". (9) He was in fact tutor to Milton Friedman, the modern guru of monetarism. Yet some of the absolutely key propositions that Simons made in his case for a properly functioning economy, especially in relation to money supply, are wholly absent in the modern version of Monetarism that has held such sway over the world's economies through the last quarter of the twentieth century.

He insisted in general terms for example, that "We should characterise as insane a government policy of alternately expanding rapidly and contracting precipitously the quantity of paper currency in circulation – as a malevolent dictator easily could do, first issuing currency to cover fiscal deficits, and then retiring currency from surplus revenues. Yet that is essentially the kind of monetary policy which actually obtains, by virtue of usurpation by private institutions (deposit banks) of the basic state function of providing the medium of circulation (and of private "cash" reserves).". (10)

His specific, key propositions for change to the monetary aspects of the system, turn up again and again in the successive essays that constitute the core of his major writings. Yet many today will find some of them to be extraordinary in the context of modern monetarism, and greatly at variance with the dominant characteristics of today's international economy in which the multinational corporations have acquired powers to rival, and increasingly to exceed, those of democratic governments.

They include for example:

1. Elimination of private monopoly in all its forms, with gradual transition to direct government ownership and operation where competition cannot be made to function effectively as an agency of control.

2. Establishment of more definite and adequate "rules of the game" with respect to money, through:

a. Abolition of private deposit banking on the basis of fractional reserves.

b. Outright federal ownership of the Federal Reserve banks and increasing concentration in the hands of central government of the power to create money and effective money substitutes.

c. Establishment of a completely homogeneous, national circulating medium and creation of a system under which a federal monetary authority has a direct and inescapable responsibility for controlling, under simple definite rules, the quantity of effective money.

d. Annulment (he suggests from a date two years after the relevant legislation) of all existing bank charters and new federal legislation providing for the complete separation, between different classes of corporations, of the deposit and lending functions of existing deposit banks.

e. Legislation requiring that all institutions which maintain deposit liabilities and/or provide checking facilities shall maintain reserves of 100% cash and deposits with the Federal Reserve banks.

f. Provision during the transitional period for gradual displacement of private-bank credit as circulating medium by credit of the Federal Reserve banks.

g. Prescription in legislation of an explicit, simple rule or principle of monetary policy, and the establishment of an appointive, administrative body (National Monetary Authority), charged with carrying out the prescribed rule, and vested with no discretionary powers as regards fundamental policy.

h. With respect to banking he suggested the replacement of existing deposit banks with two or more distinct types of institution. First, there would be deposit banks which would maintain 100% reserves, could not fail so far as depositors were concerned and could neither create nor destroy effective money. Their income would come exclusively from service charges. Second, there would be institutions similar to investment trusts which would obtain funds for lending by sale of their own stock. Their ability to make loans would be limited by the amount of funds they raised in this way.

In their total effect his various banking proposals were designed to ensure the elimination of "perverse elasticity of credit... [and for]... restoring to the central government complete control over the quantity of effective money and its value". (11) He developed in these essays proposals with a similar degree of detail in respect of Taxation, Monopoly, Merchandising (Marketing in modern parlance), Foreign Trade and Agricultural Policy etc.

We can see then from these examples, how a number of individuals of considerable standing in their own professions, including that of economics, arrived independently at a number of almost identical core ideas in their search for a remedy to the international economic crisis of the late 1920s and 1930s. Of the various proposed solutions however, it was the Keynesian prescription, which did not involve removal of the private bank monopoly of credit creation and could be accommodated to the prevailing economic and financial orthodoxies, that triumphed. The radical proposals for change to the debt-money system withered for a time on the vine and left us, with William Hixson, to consider the mystery of why "an English economist, Keynes, had such a profound influence... while a number... of economists... were expressing views of much greater theoretical soundness than he.". (12)

Alas, the Keynesian "solution" was a short lived one and the world is again facing an economic crisis which exhibits, this time in spades, all of the problems of previous economic crises.

Again the search is on for solutions. A growing number of individuals and organisations are deeply concerned to find a solution to specific problems – globalisation of trade, destruction of the environment, international debt, unemployment, drug abuse etc. Some make no direct connection between the specific problem they address and the need for any wider and truly fundamental restructuring of the current finance/economic arrangements.

Others are indeed concerned with the creation of a "New Economics" involving many interesting and potentially very important new ideas for an alternative approach to what constitutes desirable growth; how national wealth should be measured; the role of "quality of life" in that measurement etc. etc. They often appear however, to have no explicit commitment to the need for change to the debt-money system.

Yet others take a similiarly comprehensive approach to economic change but **do recognise** and insist that any lasting solution to our economic and related problems **must begin** with the radical reform of the debt-money system: the first essential step being legislation to transfer the power to create the nation's money supply from private banks to the State.

The list of such organisations would be very long. It will serve the purpose of this book however simply to make it clear, by recording a few examples, that there does exist a sound platform from which a successful popular campaign for radical reform of the finance/economic system might be launched.

THE SOCIAL CREDIT SECRETARIAT

The Social Credit Secretariat was instituted by Major C. H. Douglas in 1933 to assist him with the growing volume of international requests for information and advice. It has continued since its inception as a hierarchical organisation whose objective is to give expression to Social Credit policy and strategy. Responsibilty for this continuance was passed to his appointed Deputy Chairman on Douglas's death and the principle of responsibility by appointment in succession was thus established.

The Secretariat carries on this responsibilty for providing the authoritative guidance envisaged by Douglas, and the fundamental conception underlying the formation and continuance of the Secretariat is the avoidance of the misuse of Douglas's ideas.

Although the number of individual members and affiliated groups has fallen since the second World War there remain active Social Crediters in Britain, Australia, New Zealand and Canada. The current Chairman is based in Edinburgh, Scotland and it is from there that *The Social Crediter* and other titles, are published by the Secretariat's publishing arm, KRP Ltd. In 1994 three new booklets under the common title *Sustainable Prosperity* were published to give an up-to-date presentation in convenient form of the unchanging principles of Social Credit.

COMMITEE ON MONETARY AND ECONOMIC REFORM (COMER)

COMER was founded in Canada in 1986 by a number of eminent figures in the fields of economics, accountancy, mathematics and private business etc. They established COMER to provide "a forum for those concerned about the manifest defects of the financial system we have inherited, to debate and hopefully resolve, what can be done to change the system so that humanity can attempt to solve the problems of the real world unencumbered by a faulty financial system". (13)

Comer publishes a monthly newsletter – *Economic Reform* – and occasional scholarly papers, *The COMER Papers*. It participates in professional meetings, including many with senior politicians and civil servants. Its senior figures travel widely to support and give encouragement to monetary reformers around the world.

It also hosts an annual COMER Conference at various locations and its individual members support monetary and economic reform proposals such as the 'Sovereignty' proposal in the United States and 'Canadians for Constitutional Money' in Canada.

Its Conference in Toronto in January 1995 attracted well over 150 participants from a number of countries and speakers included its Chief Executive John Hotson, who before retirement was Professor of Economics at Waterloo University, Ontario; William Krehm, COMER Board Chairman, Mathematician and one time correspondent for *Time* magazine in Latin America; Tim Canova, Attorney in the USA and 'Visiting Scholar' in International Finance at the University of Stockholm (1988/89) and Lynn Turgeon, Professor Emeritus, Hostra University in the State of New York. A wide range of other eminent speakers included Paul Hellyer who was twice a Liberal Cabinet Minister and Jack Biddell who was "head of the largest receivership and insolvency practice in Canada... [and]... the original representative of the province of Ontario on the federal Anti Inflation Board and later as Chairman of Ontario's Inflation Restraint Board". (14)

The Conference was plainly a huge success. It demonstrated that the campaign for monetary and economic reform is increasingly broadly based and well developed, especially in Canada but in the USA too. It was also clear that discussions which are designed to refine and further develop the already detailed and practical proposals for necessary change will now be reflected in co-ordinated and effective action in North America.

NEW ECONOMICS FOUNDATION

The New Economics Foundation grew out of The Other Economic Summit (TOES) which was founded in 1984 and is held every year in parallel to the G7 nations economic summit.

The Economic Foundation itself was established in 1986 and "works to develop and promote environmentally sustainable and socially just approaches to economics". Registered as a charity, it has some 2,500 supporters in paid membership and a long list of eminent Trustees and Patrons.

It is concerned with working out "new ideas, based on the work of New

Economics pioneers like E. F. Schumacher"and it introduced to the UK in 1985, the Local Exchange Trading System (LETS), of which there are now some 270 schemes working in local communities. It has a small staff in London to undertake research and promotional work and acts to co-ordinate and organise the publication and dissemination of other relevant research. It produces quarterly, a New Economics magazine and some of its work has been released under their own titles like *The Green League of Nations, Bankwatch, Benefits and Taxes, A Radical Strategy, Trading off the Future* and *Auditing the Market.*

In 1995, on-going work included *Alternative Indicators* which recognises that "orthodox economic indicators are a poor guide to human welfare, ecological sustainability or indeed overall economic progress". (15) It has close working contact with a wide range of other organisations that are concerned with economic or environmental problems to which the New Economics are considered relevant. It does not appear however to campaign explicitly for monetary reform which would involve transfer of the power to create money from the private banking system to the state. Yet at least one paper by R. Saunders, Ecological Economist at Queensland University, recently circulated by NEF makes plain that "One of the reasons why present economies are ecologically and socially unsustainable is that the financial system locks us into economic growth...[and]... What I propose is interest free money created by the government(through the Reserve Bank) to be used to fund the construction of the infrastructural basis of a sustainable economy.". (16)

TRANSNATIONAL INSTITUTE

In one of their leaflets, The Transnational Institute (TNI) which was founded in 1973, describes itself as a "decentralised fellowship of scholars, researchers and writers from the Third World, the US and Europe committed to critical and forward-looking analysis of North-South issues, particularly in the areas of conflict, poverty and marginalisation". Initially a branch of the Institute for Policy Studies (IPS Washington DC), it is now wholly independent. It continues however to work with IPS and also works closely with institutes in Spain, Central America and the Phillipines. It has its base and a small staff in Amsterdam, from where it co-ordinates the work of some 30 fellows and associates around the world. It provides research and intellectual support for political activists, social movements and grassroots organisations, while "stimulating political and social debate transnationally in the wider society". It does this partly by organising conferences and workshops and by disseminating short papers. It has also published an extensive range of books including such titles as *The DEBT BOOMERANG, Faith and Credit, The World Bank's Empire,* and *Beyond Bretton Woods: Alternatives to the Global Economic Order.* Current research areas include Debt and International Trade, The Global Environment, Collapse of the State and Interventionism.

If we were to add to these few examples, the myriad of major single issue organisations that exist in every country in the world it must be obvious that they represent an enormous potential for radical change. To release fully that potential however, they must first come to a recognition that behind the proximate causes of the problem which is their specific interest, lies the universal root cause – the debt-money system.

It is important therefore that they be persuaded that by co-operating in a well designed international campaign, at the heart of which is reform of the money system, **they can ensure the radical monetary, economic and social changes that will deliver the specific solutions they seek.**

It is time to propose a reasonably detailed strategy and action plan for the launch and maintenance of such a campaign and this is the subject of the next and final chapter.

Notes

1.	Hattersley C. M.	1969 p. 24,84/85
2.	De Màre E.	1986 p. 111/112
3.	Burkitt B. & Hutchinson F.	1994 p. 19
4.	Soddy F.	1926 p. 108/137/138
5.	Soddy F.	1926 p. 301/302
6.	Soddy F.	1926 p. 294/304
7.	Hixson W.	1991 p. 242/244
8.	Economic Reform	1991 Vol. 3 No. 10
9.	Simons H. C.	1948 p. vi
10.	Simons H. C.	1948 p. 54
11.	Simons H. C.	1948 p. 65
12.	Hixson W.	1991 p. 122
13.	COMER Statement of Purpose	
14.	Biddell J. L.	1993 p. 9
15.	New Economics Foundation	1994
16.	R. Saunders (Paper)	

CHAPTER
9

DRAFT STRATEGY AND ACTION FOR CHANGE

1.0.0. **BACKGROUND**

1.0.1 The world's economy is in distress. The major symptoms of this distress have been rehearsed in previous chapters – long term mass unemployment; widespread poverty amidst plenty; social breakdown, increasing competition for foreign markets; a tendency to large scale war, and a human life support system that threatens to fail as the global environment is assailed by the impact of exponential economic growth.

1.0.2. But the world need not be in this condition. For at least potentially, we may choose another way. In the context of economic "growth" we have in fact three broad choices.

1.1.0. **Alternative Approaches**

1.1.1 We can accept continuous growth of output of material things on an exponential basis. This implies however a doubling and a redoubling of output again and again. A rate of growth of just 2% per year implies that total output will double every 35 years. A rate of 5% per year means it will double every 14 years. Such a process, from a base of current global output, is not sustainable for much longer and meanwhile is attended by great stress.

1.1.2 We may seek roughly linear economic growth which implies the addition of a **roughly constant** increase in a constant period of time. At relatively low annual rates of linear growth the process of growth can obviously continue for much longer. At some stage however, in a finite world, it too becomes unsustainable.

1.1.3 Finally we may seek instead, "sustainable development". Put simply the implication is that we should strive to live as far as is possible, upon the "interest" from nature's bounty rather than on its "capital". If we do that we have at least the potential to create circumstances in which our economic activity is sustainable over a very long time, and each human being may have "an equal opportunity to realise his/her potential".

1.2.0. **The Third Way**

1.2.1. We have already an economic machine with the capacity to deliver year by year a total output of goods and services sufficient to ensure a high standard of material welfare for all the world's people. By choosing "sustainable development" now therefore we have the opportunity to add **quality rather than just more material wealth, to our lives**.

1.2.2. We can devise arrangements to ensure equity (**not absolute equality**) in the distribution of goods and services. It should be accepted however that these arrangements will require, for some time, a differential approach to economic growth and some assistance to the less developed countries until there is established some reasonable degree of material equity on an international basis.

1.2.3. We can ensure the renewability of most of nature's resources – replacing what we use. We can stop damaging the natural environment and begin to repair much of the damage that has already been done.

1.2.4. We can concentrate on development related to our "spiritual" needs – social intercourse and international harmony; improvement to the democratic process and the constructive use of increasing leisure time for all with participation in the arts, sport and hobbies, debate or simply contemplation.

1 3 0. **Critical Obstacles to Change**

1 3.1. As long as the current debt-money finance system continues to drive the world's economic activity however, **we have no real choice**.

1.3.2. Exponential growth is an absolute imperative for survival of that system and it is principally through the mechanism of exponential growth that the greatest economic, social and environmental ills are inflicted upon the world.

1. 3.3. It is clear therefore, that if we are to choose the third way and the world is to escape the curse that comes with exponential growth, then the current debt-money system, critically involving money creation by commercial banks, **MUST** be radically reformed.

1.3.4. But there can be no realistic expectation that, **without massive "grassroots" pressure**, any call for such reform of that system will be supported by senior politicians who are currently, or expect to be, in positions of power.

1.3.5. There is no realistic expectation that more than a handful of career economists will be inclined, or in a position, to initiate a call for radical change to the system.

1.3.6. There is no realistic expectation that senior figures in "big business" will call for radical change to the system. Big business is always heavily in debt to the banks and relies on their goodwill.

1.3.7. Because of fear that any modification of the system that meant reduced economic growth might lead to loss of jobs, there is not even any realistic expectation that many trades unionists would be willing to take an early lead in any move to abolish the system.

1.4.0. Potential Support for Change

1.4.1. There is however a myriad of "voluntary" single issue organisations around the world with memberships that range from a few thousands to millions.

1.4.2. These organisations are concerned with specific aspects of the unfortunate fall-out from the defective economic system. If they can be persuaded that the root cause of the specific problem which motivates them is the debt-money system then some of them, even taken individually, represent a potentially powerful force for its change.

1.4.3. When however, it is more widely acknowledged that the debt-money system is **THE COMMON ROOT CAUSE** of almost all of the problems which these organisation address, the potential for a co-operative impact is very greatly increased.

2.0.0. CAMPAIGNING FOR CHANGE

2.0.1. These draft proposals reflect the urgent need to begin campaigning as quickly as is practically possible for fundamental change to the financial/economic system. For if we are to restrain the **Red Horse of the Apocalypse** and ensure at last the prospect of peace and harmony for the world's peoples, the power of banks to create money out of nothing will soon have to be withdrawn and transferred to the State.

2.0.2. They reflect the fact that there already exists a great body of important and detailed work relating to the nature of the necessary change to the debt-money system; to the setting and measuring of desirable economic objectives; and to the nature of our current democratic mechanisms.

2.1.0. **Objectives**

To establish an Economic Reform Commission whose role will be to:
      i). Organise and direct the Campaign for reform of the financial/economic system. Such change to be on the basis of transferring power and responsibilty for the creation of the national money supply from commercial banks to a statutory authority. The process must ensure that money creation will not be subject to unacceptable party political interference.

      ii). Establish and liaise at regular intervals with a wider representative consultative organisation to support, advise on and monitor campaigning action.

      iii). Establish and liaise closely with expert working groups who will produce detailed proposals for change in each of the principal areas of the Commission's remit – reform of the money system; new approaches to setting and measuring social/economic objectives and revision of the objectives and mechanics of the democratic process.

      iv). Produce a detailed Report on the agreed necessary changes and campaign for their implementation.

2.2.0. **Campaign Action Plan: First Stage**

2.2.1. Action might commence with the the formation of a small steering group whose role would be to produce a draft "constitution" and establish the Economic Reform Commission.

2.2.2. The Commission membership should ideally include senior representatives of the organisations who are most likely to provide campaigning muscle. It would be helpful also to have some credible representation from those sectors who must eventually be persuaded to act in support of change, such as politicians, economists and financial experts.

2.2.3. In the process of establishing the Economic Reform Commission and following its inauguration, the following action should be taken.
a.   Approach relevant voluntary/single-issue organisations as being potentially the most likely to recognise the need for the proposed changes to the financial/economic system, with a view to getting their agreement to:
      i. Support in principle the proposals for change and participate in the Steering Group, Economic Reform Commission, Consultative body or Working groups as appropriate.

      ii. Help fund campaigning for radical monetary change on the grounds that its success will offer the **only effective resolution** of the problem which is their special interest.

b.   Seek, in addition to funding from voluntary organisations, further funds from relevant charities and funding foundations.

2.3.0. Following the inauguration of the Economic Reform Commission, the Commission should:

i). Produce detailed Promotional Campaign proposals designed to ensure amongst the community as a whole, a sound understanding of the principles which inform the Campaign for monetary, economic and democratic change.

ii). Prepare terms of reference and establish the consultative council, and working groups.

iii). Make contact with relevant international organisations to begin a process of liaison and planning for an expansion of campaigning action on an international basis.

iv). Plan for the production of a detailed Report on the necessary changes and proposals for their carefully phased implementation.

v). Plan for a further major campaign to ensure that the Report proposals are widely understood and approved and then implemented.

BIBLIOGRAPHY

INTRODUCTION

Begg D.	1982 Rational Expectations: Revolution in Macroeconomics Phillips Allen, London.
Dernberg T. F.	1989 Global Macroeconomics Harper & Row Publishers Inc., New York.
Gordon R. J.	1990 Macroeconomics Scott, Foreman & Co. London.
Leväcic R. & Rebmann A.	1989 Macro-Economics (2nd edition) MacMillan Education Ltd., London.
Neale D.	1994 Sustainable Prosperity – A Program for Reform KRP Ltd., Edinburgh.
Ormerod P.	1994 The Death of Economics Faber & Faber, London.

CHAPTER ONE: THE DEBT – MONEY SYSTEM

Begg D. Fischer S. & Dornbusch R.	1987 Economics (2nd edition) McGraw-Hill, Maidenhead, England.
COMER	July 1994 Economic Reform Newsletter Vol. 6 No. 7 – Committee on Money & Economic Reform Toronto, Canada.
Donaldson P. & Farquhar J.	1988 Understanding the British Economy, Penguin Group, London.
Douglas C. H.	1979 The Monopoly of Credit (4th edition) Bloomfield Books, Sudbury, Suffolk.
Engdahl F. W.	1993 A Century of War Paul & Co. , Concord Mass. USA (English translation).
Hixson W.	1993 Triumph of the Bankers Preager, Westport, Connecticut & London.
Hixson W.	1991 A Matter of Interest Re-Examining Money, Debt and Real Economic Growth Preager, Westport, Connecticut, London and New York.
Hoyle J & Whitehead G.	1989 Elements of Banking Butterworth & Heinemann Oxford & London.
Levi M. D.	1990 International Finance (2nd edition) McGraw-Hill International Edition.
MacLeod H. D.	1883 The Theory and Practice of Banking Longmans Green, London.
McKenna R.	1928 Post war Banking Policy Heinemann, London.

De Màre E.   1986 A Matter of Life or Debt
                                    Veritas Pub. Co. Pty.
                                    Bullsbrook, Western Australia.
Ormerod P.   1994 The Death of Economics
                                    Faber & Faber, London.
Parkin A. & Bade R.   1988 Modern Macroeconomics
                                    Phillip Allen, Hemel Hempstead,
                                    Herts, England.
Robertson T.   1975 Human Ecology – The Science of
                                       Social Adjustment.
                                    Reprint by Christian Bookclub,
                                    California, USA.
Samuelson P. A. & Nordhaus W. D.   1989 Economics (13th edition)
                                    McGraw-Hill, International Editions.
Smith A.   1947 The Wealth of Nations
                                    Everyman's Library (reprint),
                                    J. M. Dent & Co. London.
Whitehead G.   1992 Economics (14th edition)
                                    Butterworth & Heinemann, Oxford & London.
Wonnacott P. & R.   1990 Economics (4th edition)
                                    John Wiley & Sons, New York.

CHAPTER TWO: INTERNATIONAL DEBT

Allsopp C. J. & Joshi V.   The International Debt Crisis
                                    Oxford Review of Economic Policy
                                    Vol. 2 No. 1.
Cline W. R.   1985 International Debt: Crisis to Recovery?
                                    AEA Papers & Proceedings May 1985.
Engdahl F. W   1993 A Century of War
                                    Paul & Co., Concord, Mass., USA.
George S.   1992 The DEBT BOOMERANG
                                    Pluto Press, London.
Isla A.   1993 The Debt Crisis in Latin America
                                    Canadian Women's Studies, Vol. 13 No. 3.
Levi M. D.   1990 International Finance
                                    McGraw-Hill, International Editions.
The Social Crediter   1989 KRP Ltd., Edinburgh.
                                    (Sept./Oct.)
Todaro M. P.   1989 Economic Development in
                                       The Third World
                                    Longman, New York & London.
Winters L. A.   1991 International Economics
                                    Harper Collins Academic, London.

CHAPTER THREE: ENVIRONMENTAL IMPACT

Allen R.
1992 How to Save the World
Corgi Books, London.

Annex 1
1992 Rio Declaration on Environment and Development.

Boulding K. E.
1966 The Coming of Spaceship Earth
Reader in Environmental Economics
Earthscan Publications, London.

Mishan E. J.
1969 The Costs of Economic Growth
Pelican Books, London.

Meadows D. H. & D. L.
Ronders J & Behrens W.
1972 The Limits to Growth
Pan Books, London & Sydney

Meadows D. H. & D. L. & Ronders J.
1992 Beyond the Limits
Earthscan Publications, London.

McNeill J. Winsemius P. & Yakushiji T.
1991 Beyond Interdependence
Oxford University Press
Oxford & New York.

Ormerod P.
1994 The Death of Economics
Faber & Faber, London.

Porritt J.
1990 Where on Earth are we Going?
BBC Books, London.

Slessor M.
1972 The Politics of Environment
George Allen & Unwin Ltd., London.

World Commission on Environment
1987 Our Common Future
Oxford University Press, Oxford.

CHAPTER FOUR: UNEMPLOYMENT

Evans C.
1979 The Mighty Micro
Victor Gollancz, London.

Jones B.
1982 Sleepers Wake!
Harvester Wheatsheaf, London.

Kuznets S.
1966 Modern Economic Growth
Yale University Press
Yale Connecticut, USA.

Maddison A.
1982 Phases of Capitalist Development
Oxford University Press, Oxford.

Mansfield E.
1969 Economics of Technical Change
Longman Green, London.

De Màre E.
1986 A Matter of Life or Debt
Veritas Pub. Co. Pty.
Bullsbrook, Western Australia.

Kondratief N.
1984 The Long Wave Cycle
Richardson & Snyder, New York.

International Labour Organisation Year Books

Central Statistical Office Blue Books (CSO).

1990/1994 Banking, Insurance & Finance Union Literature (BIFU).

1991 Machine Tools Statistics (MTTA).

1991 Machine Tool Enterprise(MTTA/ MTE Issue No. 4).

Scott P.	1984 Robotics Revolution
	Basil Blackwell, Oxford.
	1992 Scotsman Newspaper, Edinburgh
	1985 15th International Symposium on
	Industrial Robots, Vol. 1 of the Proceedings.

CHAPTER FIVE: SOCIAL BREAKDOWN

Crow I., Richardson P.,	1989 Unemployment, Crime and Offenders
Riddington C., Simon F.	Routledge, London & New York.
Danziger S. H. & Weinberg D. H.	1986 Fighting Poverty
	Harvard University Press
	Cambridge, Mass. USA & London.
Economist	1991 March 16th London.
Isla A.	1993 The Debt Crisis in Latin America
	Canadian Women's Studies, Vol. 13 No. 3.
George S.	1992 The DEBT BOOMERANG
	Pluto Press, London.
Goodman A. & Webb S.	1994 For Richer: For Poorer – Changing
	Distribution of Income in UK
	1961 – 1991, Institute of Fiscal studies
	(Commentary 42), London.
Harrison P.	1993 Inside the Third World (3rd edition)
	Penguin Books, London.
	1995 Herald Newspaper, Glasgow
	Icon Earth
	1995 British Broadcasting Corporation,
	London.
Myers (Ed.) N.	1994 The Gaia Atlas of Planet Management,
	Gaia Books Ltd., London.
Parker H.	1989 Instead of the Dole
	Routledge, London & New York.
Porritt J. et al.	1991 Save The Earth
	Dorling Kindersley Ltd., London.
Roll J.	1992 Understanding Poverty
	Occasional Paper 15
	Family Policy Study Centre, London.
	1995 Scotland on Sunday Newspaper,
	Edinburgh
	1995 Scotsman Newspaper, Edinburgh.
Social Trends 25	1995 Central Statistical Office.
Stevenson R.	1994 Winning the War on Drugs
	Hobart Paper 124
	Institute of Economic Affairs, London.
United Nations	1990 Global Outlook 2000
	United Nations Publications.
United Nations	1992 Year Book
	United Nations Publications.

CHAPTER SIX: SUMMARY

Gleick J.   1987 Chaos: Making a New Science
                                   Penguin, London.
Ormerod P.   1994 The Death of Economics
                                   Faber & Faber, London & Boston.

CHAPTER SEVEN: THE HISTORIC STRUGGLE FOR CHANGE

Born K. E.   1976 International Banking in the
                                      19th & 20th centuries
                                   Berg Publishers Ltd., Warwickshire.
Chorney H. , Hotson J.   1992 The Deficit Made Me Do It
  & Seccareccia M.   Canadian Centre for Policy Alternatives
                                   Ottawa, Ontario, Canada.
Douglas C. H.   1979 The Monopoly of Credit
                                   Bloomfield Books, Sudbury England.
                                   Fourth (Douglas Centenary) Edition
Douglas C. H.   1974 Economic Democracy
                                   Bloomfield Publishers, Epsom, England.
                                   (5th authorised edition).
Douglas C. H.   1933 Social Credit
                                   Eyre & Spottiswood London.
                                   (3rd edition).
Douglas C. H.   1984 The Alberta Experiment
                                   Veritas Publishing Co. Pty.
                                   Western Australia (2nd edition)
Grubiak O. & J.   1988 The Guernsey Experiment
                                   Bloomfield Books, Sudbury
                                   England (6th printing).
Hattersley J. M.   1988 Comer Paper to 14th Annual
                                   Convention of the Eastern Economics
                                      Association, Boston, Mass., USA.
                                   The Comer Papers Vol. 2
Hargreaves J.   1948 Article in Cavalcade, May 8th.
Hixson W.   1993 Triumph of the Bankers
                                   Preager Publishers, Westport, USA.
Hixson W.   1992 Henry Ford & Thomas A. Edison
                                   on Money Creation by Government
                                   COMER Papers Vol. II.
Hixson W.   1991 A Matter of Interest
                                   Re-examining Money, Debt, and
                                      Real Economic Growth
                                   Praeger, New York and London.
Krehm W.   1993 A Power Unto Itself -The Bank of Canada
                                   Stoddart Publishing Co. Ltd.
                                   Toronto, Canada.
Lekachman R.   1966 The Age of Keynes
                                   Penguin Books Ltd. Harmondsworth,
                                   England.
De Màre E.   1986 A Matter of Life or Debt
                                   Veritas Publishing Co. Pty.
                                   Bullsbrook, Western Australia.

Robertson T.

1975 Human Ecology – The Science
of Social Adjustment. Reprint
Christian Bookclub, Cal., USA.

Simons H. C.

1948 Economic Policy for A Free Society
The University of Chicago Press
Cambridge University Press
Cambridge, England.

Soddy F.

1926 Wealth, Virtual Wealth and Debt
G. Allen & Unwin, London.

CHAPTER EIGHT: SOME DETAILED PROPOSALS FOR CHANGE

Biddell J. L.

1993 A Self-Reliant Future for Canada
LNC Publications, Ontario.
(abridged edition).

Burkett B. & Hutchinson F.

1994 Major Douglas's Proposals for a
National Dividend: A Logical Successor to
the Wage
International Journal of Social Economics
Vol. 21 No. 1.

Douglas C. H.

1974 Economic Democracy
Bloomfield Publishers
Epsom, Surrey, England
(5th authorised edition).

Douglas C. H.

1921 Credit Power and Democracy
Cecil Palmer, London.
(2nd edition)

Hattersley C. M.

1969 The Community's Credit
Social Credit Co-Ordinating Centre
Mexborough, Yorks
(3rd edition).

Hixson W.

1991 A Matter of Interest Re-examining
Money, Debt and Real Economic Growth
Praeger, New York, Westport & London.

De Màre E.

1986 A Matter of Life or Debt
Veritas Publishing Company Pty.
Bullsbrook, Western Australia.
(3rd reprinting)

New Economics Foundation (NEF)

1994 Accounting For Change
NEF London.

Saunders R.

Financing the Transition to a
Sustainable Economy
Griffith University, Queensland.

Simons H. C.

1948 Economic Policy For A Free Society
The University of Chicago Press, Cambridge
University Press, Cambridge, England.

Soddy F.

1926 Wealth, Virtual Wealth and Debt
G. Allen & Unwin, London.

INDEX